THE SOUL OF A WOMAN

The Path to Healing, Love and Forgiveness

by

Daisy Arness Marrs

Enhanced DNA
DEVELOP. NURTURE. ACHIEVE.
Publishing Division

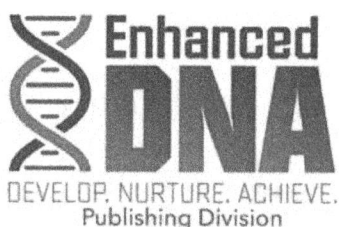

www.EnhancedDNAPublishing.com
info@EnhancedDNA1.com

THE SOUL OF A WOMAN
The Path to Healing, Love, and Forgiveness

A portion of the sales of this book will go to *A-Way-Out Ministries, Inc.*

Cover Created by Alexis Taylor (OnyxLenz.com)

ISBN-13: 978-1-7378090-6-7
Library of Congress Number: 2022918575

DEDICATION

The *Soul of a Woman* is dedicated to every woman that finally feels free about who they have become by not letting others control who they are. Those who have put past trauma behind them as they allow the will of God for their lives to move them forward. The woman that will find a partner that will accept their transformation from possession to understanding their worth because she possesses strength and wisdom. The woman that has made the change not only to put God first but themselves first, as well. The woman that knows that everything about her should be treated as a temple. The woman that understands that she does not need to be validated by anyone else to feel validated. Everything about what you want, and who you are, can be put on display for everyone to see without shame. Love your entire being so you can share the part of you that is seeking to be made whole. It is important to admire, love and nurture you by becoming an inspiration to yourself. It is the only way you can put back into the universe things that have become positive.

> *"We, as women, should be able to feel bold, beautiful, and expensive all at the same time"*

> \- Daisy Marrs

"Tell'em you are fearfully and wonderfully made, tell'em you're beautiful, tell'em nothing can stop you, tell'em you are branded by the best, tell'em you were created by the King."

- Daisy Marrs

"Feed your soul, ladies, with everything necessary to survive in order to grab hold to things that are tangible and worth saving."

- Daisy Marrs

To all of you ladies that have fought the battle to be seen and loved, you are seen.

To all the men that love all of us wholeheartedly, and treat us like ladies, thank you. The man that embraces, protects, cares, and respects the woman in us that God created us to be, we say, "Thank you for seeing our crown." *Genesis 1:27 (NIV),* says *"So God created man in his own image, in the image of God created him; male and female created he them."*

TABLE OF CONTENTS

FOREWORD vii

CHAPTER 1: THE INTRODUCTION TO BECOMING 1

CHAPTER 2: WHEN LIFE HANDS YOU LEMONS; GOD HEALS 23

CHAPTER 3: HAPPILY EVER AFTER; GOD CALLED YOU WOMAN... 31

CHAPTER 4: KNOW YOUR WORTH; COME OUT OF HIDING 41

CHAPTER 5: A WOMAN ACTIVATED; THE SOUL OF A WOMAN... 49

CHAPTER 6: A SEAT AT THE TABLE................................... 57

CHAPTER 7: STAY IN YOUR NOW; LOVE DEPENDS ON IT .. 69

CHAPTER 8: EMPOWERED AND BEYOND 77

CHAPTER 9: SPEAKING TO MY YOUNGER SELF; MY FIRST LOVE.. 83

CHAPTER 10: THE UNDOING OF EVERY ATTACK................. 93

CHAPTER 11: ONE LIFE TO LIVE 99

CHAPTER 12: STEPPING INTO MY NEW *THANG*; WHEN A WOMAN IS FED UP 107

CHAPTER 13: A STRANGER IN MY HOUSE 113

CHAPTER 14: I BEAR MANY FACES; BECOME THE BRAND 117

CHAPTER 15: LIFE IS JUST A REHEARSAL; FINAL CURTAIN CALL.. 123

ABOUT THE AUTHOR.. 131

FOREWORD

Healthy personhood is essential to developing a heart which can positively impact society. It is through the well-nourished heart that we properly define experiences and transfer the benefits gained in life's triumphs to others with similar histories. A woman with a heart filled with the powerful and positive lessons of what God has brought her through is not only valuable to society but even more precious to God. In Daisy Marrs' latest gift to humanity entitled The Soul of a Woman! The Path to Healing, Love and Forgiveness, we find pages filled with what it means to learn from trial and triumph and how God makes the most impactful women in our world.

Women around the globe have a deep and rich history of subjugation and being deprioritized. It is my belief that for the five components of the soul to lead us into the greatest expression of ourselves we must, as Ms. Marrs explains, "prioritize ourselves" to become the best version of ourselves. The soul comprised of the mind, will, emotion, imagination and intellect, needs experiences to become a wise unit within our ontology. This book helps to unify the components of the soul so that they begin to work more in tandem with women's call from God to transcend any moment while simultaneously thriving in every hour.

I highly recommend this book to every woman seeking to transcend and overcome the categorizing that can so easily hinder potential. This book provides a portable and sustainable outline for women seeking to accomplish all that life's experiences, pains, struggles and victories have put them in position to use to be epic for themselves and all women who would seek to be empowered!

Clyde Posley, Jr., D.D, Ph.D.
Moderator,
Union District Baptist Association
Senior Pastor, Antioch Baptist Church
Indianapolis, IN

CHAPTER 1: THE INTRODUCTION TO BECOMING

After years of abuse, it was time to move forward. But first I had to complete one final step: my divorce. I was preparing to adjust to my new normal because I was no longer feeling vulnerable and distracted. I had to remind myself that I am a woman of strength who had survived an initial life-threatening situation. I was twenty-seven years old, and it felt like the weight of the world had been lifted off my shoulders; from all the years of physical pain, and the staggering fog of mental abuse that had weighed me down.

Now that the fog was about to be lifted, I wanted to meet myself. The introduction to myself would be like no other because this was like a meet and greet session to me. This would be the first time I would meet the actual person outside of someone else's power, so to speak, because I was bound by the spirit of abuse, but set free as a child of God. What a wonderful feeling! After all, I was about to be divorced, and officially about to hold the title of *single mother*. Although this title does not represent what a whole family should look like, it would become my greatest honor. My daughter deserved to live a peaceful life without the distractions of abuse surrounding her. In addition to this, I wanted to know how this view of the world looked from my daughter's eyes at six years old. Did she feel like I did when I witnessed abuse at her age? Also, is she proud of me for getting the two of us out of it, and is she proud of the woman that raised her? The answer to these questions was an astounding, yes. As an adult woman, she can now express all that concerned her as a child, but she was always proud of me. How is it that our lives were so similar at her age, and why didn't I recognize it from the start?

Becoming blind to my physical state kept me from recognizing the obvious; but I was now able to come to terms with and enjoy all that life had to offer. Considering I was preparing to be free in order to adjust to my circumstances, I could look at myself through a healed lens and allow myself full transparency with my thinking. Meaning, I couldn't try and justify anything that had happened to me up to this point, but I had to accept the outcome. When you do this, you can then accept your transition. This was the only way to move forward in a positive way; because without acknowledging your past, you can't change for your future. You will actually lie dormant in it until you do.

So, to be honest with myself or anyone reading this, I was a total disaster. I was walking through life without giving any thought to fooling anyone since my life had been displayed in full view. I was fully able to understand that I couldn't remove the pain that was in my life, but I could rotate it and adjust it to fit my life now. However, it would take years of understanding and trying to figure myself out and it would take a while to remove the stigma of shame that followed me around. It was like a shadow that followed me everywhere I went in which darkness would direct my path. Allowing myself to climb into my own headspace helped me to materialize what life should be and understand that no one else is allowed there.

I'm now a sensational woman visualizing her own future while evolving brilliantly from her past. Everything about me is full of excitement because I now control today. Ultimately, realizing in my own mind that I was safe, helped me to evolve into the woman I am today. That's right, protect your psyche at all costs, because if you don't, you will be drawn into dealing with someone else's thoughts of you. So, what would become my perception of everything that I had gone through? Discovering my worthiness was more than just looking at myself from my point of view, because I had to see myself as God saw me. *Psalm 139:13-14 (NIV)* states, *"For you created my innermost being; you knit me together in my mother's womb. I praise you because I am fearfully and wonderfully made; your works are wonderful; I know that full well."* So, this means I could see myself as God made me which was what I needed to do in order to fulfill who I was to be.

I remember one day, while in the abusive relationship, I was outside washing my car and I had a black eye. I can't remember what transpired the night before that brought the abuse on, but my entire body was fully affected by it. I also recall painfully bending over to clean up my car, the anger that I had, and thinking I will not let what happened keep me from being present in the moment. It's important to understand that there is never a reason for abuse, and it's never your fault, but fault stares you in the face like staring in a mirror; constantly giving yourself a startling view of yourself. Anyway, at that moment, there was anger instead of love for that relationship, and fear instead of peace as I thought about how I felt.

As I think back, "What gave me the strength to endure the pain and keep moving as if nothing had happened to me?" *How could I even perform as a woman in a society with so much brokenness inside?* In addition, what gave me the courage to show up in front of others wearing the bruises as if they were badges of honor?

I'm remembering my mother at this time because she had so much strength during times of abuse when she should have broken down and simply given up. Instead, she rose up and showed herself in spite of it all. The fearful little girl inside her stood up to the man that said she couldn't do it all alone. She unknowingly passed the baton to me. Had abuse become our foundation or did our foundation become the abuse? How can you ever tell the two apart?

Anyway, I recall a friend of my exes walking past me that day while I was cleaning my car, and looking me in the eyes, but saying absolutely nothing. The shame and disgust I felt in that moment is unexplainable. However, I have come to understand that many people are enablers of abuse, and some don't even realize it. Or do they? Because he saw my face and said nothing. Had I gotten so used to the attacks that it actually became who I was? Nope, I had to show up for myself and my daughter in order to get to the next phase of our lives. Indeed, during that time in my life, God was preparing me for something greater.

That very day, even while in pain and not even realizing it, I was becoming a new person because I still stood ten toes down in spite of it all. I felt that young girl inside my mother become the strength in me. To become all that I could be by not allowing the downfall that men saw us as, strengthen me. God was preparing me for purpose. It was an introduction to myself like no other, and I was now prepared to greet myself with the love for which I longed. I figured out that learning to spend time alone was my superpower; meditation is essential. You have to admire yourself in your own love language. Invest in yourself as if you are the most valuable player. Ask yourself this simple question: how do you introduce yourself to someone that has been a complete stranger? I had to do this myself. After all, I was in my early twenties when the realization hit me that I was greater than the situation.

As I reflect back, I can see a woman desperately struggling to be free even earlier. The body that was abused in so many ways was transforming in a beautiful way. Life in that body was so full of adversities. Based not only on how it responded to situations, but how it reacted to what life had handed down to it, was scary at best. Who was this woman that had survived life against all odds? The woman that was disowned, abandoned, mistreated, misguided, and in a small way, a total stranger without an identity. My identity was snatched away from me at birth. Yes, this white-looking baby with no hair on her head entered into a world with a purpose without even knowing it. Being disowned by my father left a major question lingering in my mind. If I was not my father's child, then who was I? Becoming accustomed to those words was a challenge. Strangely enough, my daughter's father had said the same thing about her that my father had said about me, "She is not my child!"

Anyway, the man who had fathered me had forgotten that he was supposed to protect me and be the role model that would teach me how to move forward in life. Instead, he left me to figure out life all by myself after the damage he had bestowed upon me. Although as a young child, I could not explain the impact my father had on me; he shaped my life from the very beginning. Why is it that all I can remember are the bad things that occurred from my father, and hardly anything good at all? Could it be that there was not much good that came from the relationship with him?

I remember years ago my father sent for me and my sisters to visit him and his new family; he had remarried after he and my mother had divorced. He had previously only sent for my older sister to visit him but decided to invite my younger sister and me this time. I was about eight or nine years old when we visited him and his new family in Cleveland, Ohio. I was so excited. We got to meet his new family, but I continued to feel the disconnect from him; but it did not matter because I was in his presence. I was feeling jealous though, because his new family was experiencing something with him that I never got to experience; being a family. I also recall him taking us to see a nightclub where he worked so that we could meet some of the people working there while he took care of some business. This is of importance to me because I mattered in that moment. Although the business was closed because it was outside of business hours, I was a part of the visit. We were able to go inside and look around and meet some people that were preparing for the evening. He introduced us, and to hear him say, "These are my daughters," was an indescribable feeling. He even took us shopping for new clothes while visiting. I was able to see a part of him that I never experienced before. The excitement of my father doing something for me was pure joy. My sisters and I were able to pick out a few new outfits. This would be the only time I could remember him buying me something after my parents divorced. However, his new wife wasn't pleased with the purchase; so, the next morning when we woke up, the new outfits had been returned to the store. This was confusing, because this, to me, was a time that he should have fought for us, but he did not. I do recall how disappointed and sad my sisters and I were. This was my only view of how his wife treated us; I wasn't made to feel as comfortable as I should have been during our visit. However, at the time, my focus was on my father, not my stepmother. He was an important person to everyone that knew him, at least that's how it appeared to me. I always saw him as a perfect man; even the way he dressed and carried himself was classy. He always wore hats that would match everything he wore as they were a part of his style. Funny, I am that way today; except with me, its glasses, so I guess I got that from him without knowing it. I can see him so clearly…dancing to one of his favorite songs by Tyrone Davis, called, "Can I Change My Mind?" while he did a dance called the Camel Walk. I smile at that memory every time I think about it. When I hear that song today, I think of him and see him dancing with his skinny legs.

Anyway, my father also had a smile that would light up the room. I wish he and I could have had a conversation before his death so my heart could have healed from my childhood trauma. But instead, I had to release and let go. That is one of my biggest regrets. There were so many questions I had that were left unanswered.

I have a photo that I hold dear to my heart; it is of my father with me and my sisters while we were in Cadiz, Kentucky, my hometown, for my brother's funeral when I was in my early twenties. We were at my grandmother's house standing in her front yard when the photo was taken. He, like us, came to town for our brother's funeral; his son. As I reflect back on the picture, I can remember the joy I felt in standing with him. Although he appeared to be happy to see me, there was really no real connection between us. However, the excitement I felt just being near him is unexplainable. The little girl that had been abandoned needed to feel something at that moment, though. I don't think I realized at the time how he treated me or if I even cared when I was younger. I just enjoyed the moment. Unfortunately, I have now come to understand that during that very time, I was in a stage of abuse; so, I would not have recognized the disconnection as I should have. I wish I could have felt comfortable in sharing my circumstance with him, but if I had, would he have even cared? Because of the shame of what I was going through at that time, I had even hidden the abuse from my family.

It's funny, but we were all home again together for the first time since he had relocated our family from Kentucky to Indianapolis many years before. Now I am starting to remember other things that affected me during that moment. Such as when visiting Cadiz as a young girl, I would hear people talking about my sisters and me being his children because we were very young when we left, so they were starting to remember us. So, on the day with him present, we were able to stand with him as his children in our hometown to be seen by everyone. It was such a pivotal moment, I think, for all of us. I remember standing proud with my sisters when we attended our brother's funeral and being acknowledged as his children because no one at home had seen us together with him since I was about three or four years old. Many of us, that have been abused, forget during moments like this, about ourselves and how others make us feel because we want to please others. So, anything negative that happened would be momentarily forgotten. This was one of my people-pleasing moments because I didn't think about how my father made me feel growing up. All I cared about was that I was in his presence at that moment.

I have since learned that this is not enough and is totally unacceptable. We must want validation for ourselves as much as we validate someone else. *It is never okay to become invisible to someone else's truth.* Therefore, don't let embedded fear hide or control your present moment. My fear of my father was forgotten at that moment because he gave me some of the attention that I had craved. However, during the time with my father in Kentucky, we were complete strangers even though I had his blood running through my veins. At that time, I was fighting for my identity because I wanted people to know that he was my father. However, the disconnect he had for me from birth, gave way to a dysfunctional relationship between us that will last me a lifetime. So, attention given will not calm the beast that had raised up against me. It only provides them the courage to continue the attacks against you. Ultimately, what we allow will continue with no chance for change and can show up in other relationships. We can't continue to put ourselves in a position to be wronged. Therefore, introducing yourself to self-care is absolutely a must. Self should be at the top of the list in every situation, but not the self that shows up in the physical, as it has to be pulled from within. It has to be all mental in order for you to protect yourself and your mental strength. So, when should you start thinking about the life that has finally caught up with you? Will you evaluate everything that happened to you or simply let it go?

As I reflect back, I remember seeing another photo of myself in our home in Cadiz when I was about two or three years old. My hair was in little ponytails all over my head in this black and white photo that I cherish because that is the only photo I have of myself. I was standing in the front yard of our home in Kentucky. So, I get to wonder what I looked like as I aged; although, in my mind, I see myself growing through the years as a slightly sad, shy little girl because of the vivid memories of how my father treated me.

Now it was time to get to really know me. It was hard to imagine that figuring out myself was such a serious task; I had to put all my focus on it. First, I understood I had to act as if I had never met myself before because nothing in my life was ever really about me. Indeed, my life had been attached to someone else's identity and how they perceived me; so, pressing forward would be hard. It is so important to disconnect from someone else's betrayal in order to destroy what has impacted you mentally. In many ways, my identity was attached to someone else and how they treated me or acted towards me, and this helped shape who I had become. I am stronger because of it. Mary J. Beige said it best, "I'm so tired of feeling empty, dry my eyes it's time to fight," in a song written as an anthem to herself, and without realizing, it became one for many of us. Those words resonate with many of us that have found ourselves fighting to just be us. The tears we have cried are basically lonely tears as we fight our way through while sitting in silence. We have to become more than what others see. So, I started off by admiring all the attributes that were before me. This body that was once beaten and bruised needed to be reshaped and molded into the beautiful person God created it to be.

So, you must ask yourself; What features do you want to see in this person? How would you want your character to be portrayed? Would you be happy staying with this person for a lifetime? How would you show up on a date with yourself? How can anyone represent themself unless they know who they are. It can be like completing a resume of yourself, and yes, asking yourself a lot of questions is a must. You must put down all that you have done, or have allowed done, to you and then present it back to yourself. Then after all that, accept who you are.

I started to take myself out on dates to see what I liked, and what I did or did not enjoy about myself, in order to accept what others had to give. For so long, a narrative about who I was had been created by people that ultimately controlled my life. The book of *Lamentation 3:22-23 (NIV)*states, *"Certainly the faithful love of the Lord hasn't ended; certainly, God's compassion isn't through! They are renewed every morning. Great is your faithfulness."* Therefore, when you look to the creator of the universe and realize that He created you because He loved you, it puts a different perspective on your thinking because He is faithful.

I still continue dating myself to this very day. I tell you, everything about that date is wonderful, and I sit there and enjoy myself for hours. I had to learn to love how I showed up for myself and celebrate who I came to be. While discovering my very being, I figured out It was okay to welcome people in while putting provisions on their entry; setting boundaries on them. In addition, I have learned not to let them get too comfortable because it is then that you will be taken for granted most of the time. So, ask yourself; how will you show up? It is an awesome experience being able to create my own atmosphere by not allowing others to dictate my every move.

Finally, after all that, I got to meet the person that had longed to surface for such a long time. I was very humbled by God's grace in how He allowed me to show up. Suddenly, the very one that would peep out every now and then started to emerge. She stepped out in a very unique way. Her speech had changed because the vulgar language that used to come out of her mouth did not represent the person that she had become. I cursed often, so I thought, how is this becoming of a young lady that chose to leave behind all of who she was? Indeed, the words that flowed from my mouth, in terms of how I used them, had to change because they were so damaging to those that heard them. I had to re-evaluate everything about me, so I made a mental checklist of things I was no longer going to do or say. I had to find my God story; you know the one that helps you shine brightly, and helps you move forward without shame. Yes, that one. I was the one that would approve me. The one that would become that perfect light in guiding me on a magnificent journey. Ultimately, her beauty was enhanced by what was no longer there. Even the scars that came with her had to be presented in a different way because they could not bring the emotions with them. The introduction to myself was not only highlighted by whom God said I was, but who I had found along the way.

Finding myself was a major discovery; as I began to think, how was it possible that I had been on this earth for 27 years and was never given the privilege to know who I was. Once you figure out that you can be the best of yourself, then the greatest version will show up. The life prior to this moment no longer had a hold on me. I was becoming a lady right before my very eyes. However, before this day would come, I had to complete that final chapter.

Yep, you guessed it; the divorce. All the in between stories would have to be dissolved with this final chapter, and that included the separation from my father. Finalizing this chapter in my life would ultimately help bring out the best in me. I had to finalize the divorce from the man that had tormented me for such a long time. That crazy life of trying not to step on a time-bomb, as if I was in a war zone, had to officially come to an end. The day the judge granted my divorce was a day of long-awaited rejoicing. It was a long road getting there, but there I was for the first time, seeing my way through. However, I was also plagued, during this time, with fear of not knowing if I would survive my court appearance. After almost losing my life when filing for divorce, I was finally there. I gently smile now thinking about that moment because the brave part of me showed up; you know the one that stood ten toes down. All the drama leading to this day had to come to an end.

Unfortunately, in the days leading up to the divorce hearing, I found myself in a complete panic. I was completely terrified. Each day of waiting would bring a different feeling as I was so excited to put my past behind me. However, I had to be reminded that there was one step left: the final step. "The divorce papers have officially been sent out," my attorney informed me via phone, and they were delivered to a known address where my then-husband was staying since we were no longer together due to the legal separation. What I didn't know was what his immediate reaction would be to the date that was on the papers he had received. Almost losing my life because of a set of papers being delivered before, into the hands of a man that dominated my existence, was devastating enough, yet I survived. This time was really different because the separation was shifting. I was now more terrified than before. This would be our last communication in terms of court appearances. Those papers would continue a spiral in my life that was as dangerous as when I filed for a legal separation. Because in my exe's eyes, they were basically the same; I was leaving him.

However, to me, it was a time of reflection to start the beginning of my life. Yes, the day that I had been longing for to fight for my freedom was finally here. I remember getting up very early in the morning feeling happy after a restless night, but fearful at the same time, if that, indeed, could be possible. My feelings were all over the place, and yes, my dreadful friend, anxiety, was tagging right along with me. My mind kept thinking about this being the most dangerous time in my life, after all the other dangerous moments, as I was coming to the end of the relationship that somehow stole a major part of me. We must remember leaving an abusive relationship is the most dangerous time for anyone trying to be free. Although, when looking back at what happened to me when filing the legal separation-papers, it tormented me for some time because this was torture. Therefore, when making the decision to end years of torment, I had to be prepared for the continued fight to save my life. I had been told what would happen if I filed for divorce, but that did not make it any easier. I had told one of my sisters if something were to happen to me, please take care of my daughter. The closer the time came for me to appear in court for the hearing, the more my heart started to pound. As everything was starting to become real, my palms started sweating, my hands shaky, and I felt a sense of dread come over me while somehow feeling disconnected. In the mirror, as I was getting myself together and putting my makeup on, I saw a very strong, beautiful black woman with a smile that lit up through the mirror. She was speaking to herself, saying, "You got this." However, my body was saying something completely different.

Outside that very mirror was this broken little girl who was trying to break free and needed her father during this time. He had still not been a part of her life. My body was weak as I recognized the fear that was taking hold of me at that very moment. This was to be the day that I could break the chains that had broken me, but somehow, I could not see past the present moment. How is it that all the years of abuse were staring me right in my face as they came racing toward me all at once? I had to shake it off, get myself dressed, and realize that this day would be the beginning of the rest of my life. I even put on a brand-new outfit to mark the occasion.

The life God had predestined for me was waiting. It was as if God at that very moment said to me, "I am with you." *Deuteronomy 31:8 (NIV) says, "The Lord himself goes before you and will be with you; he will never leave you nor forsake you. Do not be afraid; do not be discouraged."* I had to make myself remember that God has always been with me.

I *was* preparing to walk out the door when suddenly the phone rang, and I became startled. The voice on the other end made me feel at ease as he knew my fear. I was afraid that once I showed up at the courthouse, my life would be in danger. Then the voice on the other end reassured me that I would be just fine. I suddenly felt a sense of calm as I thought about God shielding me and about the voice He sent to calm me. The next call I received was from my attorney, making sure that we would meet at our expected location and time at the courthouse. He was also reassuring me that the divorce would be final on this day, and everything would be fine. I prayed that my legal separation would officially be over because it had been over two years, and that my divorce would be final.

Driving down to the courthouse was unreal; the longer I drove, the longer it seemed to take. I was asking God to shield me and protect me. Have you ever faced the unknown? Well, this was a day of the unknown for me, simply because I didn't know what stood before me. I did not want to make that drive, and I wished my attorney and the judge could have finalized my divorce without me being there. I distinctly remember getting out of my car and looking all around. I was surveying my surroundings. "Is he out here somewhere?" I thought. He could be waiting for me outside the courthouse determined to stop this divorce, and to take my life, as he had tried before. "My life is in danger," I thought to myself, as I felt all alone. In fact, I was all alone and felt like law enforcement should have been with me because of the past abuse. I kept thinking, "God is with me," over and over in my head. I felt the presence of God with each step that I took toward the courthouse. However, when I had made it inside the building in one piece, I thought, "God, this is so hard." Going through this type of fear is so real even when you feel the presence of God. I kept taking my mind off of Him and putting it on my situation which is something I have grown not to do since then. So, I was tormenting myself with what I viewed as a real threat at the time. The human part of me was full of dread, and it seemed to be one of the longest walks I had ever taken. It was like I was in some type of horror movie because the stretch of the sidewalk seemed to get further and further away as I walked. My pace could not have been fast enough. Once I found myself in the courthouse, there were so many people. I concentrated on everyone, every door, and every corner of the building. Since I didn't encounter him outside, could he be waiting for me on the inside of the City-County Building? There had been so many incidents where a perpetrator had killed the person that had made up their mind to get to this step. So, I was very attentive to everything, my surroundings, and every person that walked my way. What could I have done though had he been waiting for me? Could I have even protected myself? I was a perfect target during that situation because I was all alone walking into the courthouse. I honestly think that someone should meet individuals going to court for domestic violence incidents at all times because of the danger.

Anyway, I finally saw my attorney near the courtroom door where we were to meet, and I felt some type of relief. We did not see my ex-husband at all as we waited to be called inside the courtroom. We were able to talk about the proceedings, and to what he would or would not object. I can honestly say I had chosen a good attorney because he was my biggest, and only, advocate. Finally, my name was called, and we went inside the courtroom. I still had not seen my ex-husband. The judge proceeded to have my attorney and me come forward in his presence. All I could think about was, "where was he?" It was time for me to come face to face with the person that had tried to take my life. It was time for me to face the man who had abused and stalked me for a major part of my life. However, he was nowhere to be seen. Here I am, finally in the courtroom, feeling a sense of relief because of not having to see him, but hoping that his not showing up would not impede my divorce. Worrying, I started to ask my attorney a lot of questions since we did not see him. He assured me that we were good. Fortunately, the judge proceeded without him. My divorce was finalized without him being there. I couldn't capture into words how I felt at that very moment. "Your divorce is granted," the judge said. He said, just because he did not show up, did not mean that the divorce proceeding wouldn't go on. The judge then said to my attorney and me that the proceedings for the divorce hearing that were delivered to the address on file, were signed, received and returned with a signature from someone at the home in which he was living. The final divorce papers will be delivered to that same address. My attorney then translated it to mean that he was, and will be, notified of the final divorce. Not showing up did not stop the divorce; I am sure he thought it would not proceed.

I went into a silent dance. I rejoiced as tears flowed down my face. It was a long journey getting here. Everything that my attorney had asked for was granted which included a restraining order for life from seeing our child unless he provided to the court proof of required classes. I did not know how I would feel being single and free. After all, my entire life someone else was controlling me. How was I supposed to act now that I was divorced? How should I be feeling now that I am divorced?

I have come to understand that was the first day of the rest of my life. Somehow, I felt I was set free from my father, as well, and all the trauma he had caused me. So, I also mentally divorced him that day and every man that caused me trauma growing up as a child. When I signed all the documents the judge handed me and my attorney, all I heard was, "You are now *free*." My attorney then gave me the biggest hug. He knew the struggles I had been through because he had been there with me the entire time with my court dates. He fought for me, and I appreciate him more than anything. He was the first man that ever fought for me, and I promised myself that no man would ever dismiss me again. The judge, I am sure, didn't understand or appreciate my joy because so many others like me come before him for various reasons. I survived for this day and was able to see it through. From the very moment of my divorce, I felt emboldened to be the person God created me to be. I had moved beyond my past the moment the judge granted my divorce, and I walked right into what God had for me.

The divorce papers were mailed to the same address informing my ex-husband of the divorce being final, as well as all that I was entitled to have in the end. Honestly, I did not care about any of the material things because my freedom was worth its weight in gold.

That very day, I Introduced myself to someone I never knew, and although it took me a while to get to know her, it was all worth the wait. Nobody really knows me because I didn't really know myself. Each day that God gives me, I am learning a new me. I'm embracing the new woman that God shows her she is each day, and all the ghosts from my past can no longer haunt me because of what I saw as a child or endured growing up. Even the nasty old man next door that touched me as a young girl no longer had a hold on me. To not change, is to stay stagnant from who God created you to be; but to forgive, is a gift that not many can do. Learn to move past your challenges by not dying in the process. Just like the plants that have not been watered stop growing and die, so will you, if you don't replenish yourself every day. I am no longer the woman of yesterday, but a woman of that change. This should be the mindset of everyone in order to reach your highest potential in life so you can manifest into your best self. Mature yourself and manifestation will come. Allow yourself to bridge the gap between your now and your future self, while introducing you to the best part of you. Never let man define who you are because God already has.

Reflection: Be beautiful, be bold, be intentional about life. Yearn to let go of your yesteryears in order to find what has awakened you today. Lust over yourself so the lust of what's felt inside can embolden you to be free. *Luke 8:17 (KJV) "For nothing is secret, that shall not be made manifest; neither (anything) hid, that shall not be known and come abroad."*

CHAPTER 2: WHEN LIFE HANDS YOU LEMONS; GOD HEALS

Women oftentimes feel we are the ones that carry the greatest burdens. We are the ones that stay up all night praying over our children when they aren't feeling well. The one's that take care of our homes and are ever-present. Life is hard at times. But, how we step into it is rewarding, once we realize how we accept each moment presented to us as we embrace them tightly. Women have come to realize that even in our weakest moments, God gives us strength. Loving all of who we are is essential in order to have a resourceful life, good or bad. We must understand that our tests and trials can become our most triumphant moments. I also believe that through our forgiveness of others, God forgives us. And we then reap His promises, no matter the damage done to us. *Jeremiah 30:17 (KJV) says, "For I will restore health unto thee, and I will heal thee of thy wounds, saith the Lord…"* So, we must forgive others that have wronged us in order to reap the harvest of God, even in all the burdens we carry. Forgiving ourselves is also an important task. It's because of me forgiving others, according to *Matthew 18:22 (NIV)*, even if it's more than once, that I believe God continuously shows up for me in my life. Even when I came across all those sour patches, and believe me, they were many I forgave. Although it was hard to get to the moment of forgiving myself because I was angry, it was necessary in order to heal.

In sharing another time when life tried its best to give me lemons, I will reflect on March 18, 2018, as a day I will never forget. It's funny how I can now say I will never forget, because on that particular day, at some point and time, I could not remember. Reflecting back on that day, I had to be told what happened to me. It was on a Sunday, and I was at church and had just led our praise and worship team in song. It was a day of reflection as I was told something wasn't quite right when I was singing. The words to the song weren't coming to me as usual; so, why didn't I realize that something was off? It was as if I was moving in slow motion, so to speak. However, when I finished the song, I took my seat and participated in the rest of the service without incident, or so I thought. Yep, my body was starting to go through a physical change, and I didn't realize it at the time. Anyway, when leaving the church with my husband, I recall telling him I felt funny, but really nothing else out of the ordinary stuck-out to me. In addition, I had no idea that the church that I stood in front of, singing that day, noticed something different when I was singing, and it wasn't until I returned to church that I was made aware of it. It was a typical Sunday morning, and I would leave my home to go pick up one of my grandsons because he loved going to church with us. There appeared to be nothing out of the ordinary at the time. However, after leaving the church, I went home to lay down to rest for a while. A few days later, I woke up in the hospital, not realizing when I had gotten there or why I was there. Time had actually stood still. During that time, I have no recollection of the days during my hospitalization; so, everything I am sharing, was told to me.

We must understand that when God has his hands on you, everything about you is covered by His blood. When you believe in His word, you reap abundantly. Scripture says, "*If you believe, you will receive whatever you ask for in prayer*", *Matthew 21:22 (NIV)*. You must also stay in prayer daily, as well, and believe what you pray for because you will never know when your prayers will need to be answered. So, consistently stay in prayer to cover yourself.

Anyway, I was facing a new trial in my life because of my health. I now understand that life tried to hand me another bad batch of lemons as Satan had me under yet another attack. My body was under attack again, and I didn't realize it. I was facing something that almost cheated me out of purpose. According to www.LearningEnglish.voanews.com "the word lemon represents something poor, bad or broken. A 'lemon' can also mean an unsatisfactory answer." There was something bad going on regarding my health, and no one was sure of the outcome. Although, God knew my outcome, the doctors and my family did not at the time. As my symptoms were getting worse, they had no idea where things were headed. My daughter shared with me that while at home, lying in my bed prior to being hospitalized, I asked my grandson how he got to our home. This question to him would start a chain of events. Right away he noticed something wasn't quite right and called his mother, my daughter, telling her that something was wrong with me because I did not remember picking him up; without hesitation, she came to my house. Keep in mind, from the moment I left the church and laid down, my grandson never left my side. In fact, he sat in a chair in my bedroom right next to the bed. I was told that when my daughter arrived, I was talking about my blood pressure, and was trying to take medication. My daughter started to question me but also noticed I was not myself. I became argumentative as she tried to take the medication bottles out of my hands because I had told her that I had already taken my medication earlier. She was not going to allow me to take any more medication for fear that I would overdose. During this moment, she shared that pills went all over the room as she tried taking the pill bottles out of my hand as I resisted. She also told my grandson to call 911 for medical assistance because I was exhibiting symptoms that needed immediate attention, and as a nurse, she knew something wasn't quite right. The police arrived first, and she tried to keep me calm as she spoke to the officers explaining what was going on with me, and not allowing them to think I was under the influence of something. They immediately thought I was on drugs as my daughter was explaining to them that I did not do drugs and that something was medically wrong. The ambulance arrived shortly afterward, and I was told that I was able to walk to the ambulance while being assisted onto a gurney by the attendants. My vital signs were assessed, and because my blood pressure had reached a dangerous point, lights and sirens were immediately activated, and I was transported to a nearby emergency room. When arriving, medical personnel took over and initiated the stroke protocol due to my elevated blood pressure and disorientation to person, place, and time. My family arrived immediately behind me as they had to drive their personal vehicles. They were fearful and very concerned of what was going on with me. Once in the hospital, they were also questioned by medical personnel about me taking any illegal drugs because they were preparing to run blood tests.

The first thing that the doctors had to do was control my blood pressure and bring my numbers down as quickly as possible. Intravenous therapy was initiated so that medications could be given immediately. My family was present and, as my husband stood by my bedside, the nurses were asking my daughter questions. A particular nurse asked my daughter if I had taken anything that would have me in the state that I was in, and this nurse was sure I had taken some type of illegal drug. Angrily my daughter answered, saying, "My mother does not do drugs." She informed me that the nurse gave her a look as if she didn't believe her as she prepared to gather urine to obtain a drug screen. My daughter stood firm with a nurse that was pretty sure that when my urinalysis results came back, it would be positive for illegal drugs. This is a strange reaction from medical personal. However, when all my results returned negative for drugs, no apology was offered to my daughter or family.

Many tests were performed; like CAT Scans, MRIs, and numerous blood draws which ultimately ruled out a stroke. It would take a few days for me to return to my normal state, and I am so thankful for my grandson and daughter for their immediate attention because without their assistance, the outcome would have been much different. Ultimately, on discharge from the hospital, a diagnosis of Hypertensive Encephalopathy was given. The dictionary says this is due to increased cerebral perfusion from the loss of blood-brain barrier integrity, which results in the exudation of fluid into the brain.

God kept me that day, and I believe my grandson was used to assist me in my time of need because, normally, I would take him home after church. At the time, I could not remember the month, day, or name of the President of the United States. The medical professionals used drastic measures that day. After a few days of being in the hospital, and numerous tests being ran over several days, I started to be myself again. When I left the hospital after being there for five days, all tests were negative, and I was back to myself. The devil and all his fiery darts could not keep me down; God healed me that day as he has numerous times before. He has kept me through numerous car accidents; a couple of them nearly took my life. One, in which I nearly lost my daughter when she was four years old, we were ran off the road by another vehicle. Immediately after that accident, I had to initiate the Heimlich maneuver on her as I noticed her start to lose consciousness due to a blockage in her airway. We hit a light pole while my daughter was eating, and some of it had gotten lodged in her throat. Blood was running down my face and all over me because my forehead was busted wide open, and even though nerves had been cut, God kept me alert enough to save her. He is always there for me holding me up and being my strength. He gives me the power to step forward when I think that there is none of me left to give.

The journey that I have lived lets me know that God wants to not only heal, but save us. *Exodus 15:26 (AMP) says, "For I am the Lord who heals you."* In addition, *Psalm 147:2 (NIV) says, "He heals the brokenhearted and bandages their wounds."* What this scripture tells me is that God not only heals us, but He wants us healed. He wants us to live in our purpose. He is always there to comfort us even when we don't think He's there. Through all the obstacles that you think are there to hold you back; your past traumas, abandonments, and even through all the paths of life we take, our hearts and souls can be healed. We are to continue pushing forward no matter what. God can heal all our pain, even when we, as women, have been deeply hurt or think we have been left all alone...if we just believe in His word. Remember, He loves us and is always there to protect us just as we protect our children. Scripture says, *Roman 5:8 (LEB) "But God demonstrates His own love for us in this: While we were still sinners, Christ died for us."* As God protects us in our darkest moments, remind yourself to always put prayer in your day to day talk with Him. You have to be your biggest advocate to Him. Let it be the catalyst that draws you to your healing as you face the challenges of life because they will come.

Reflection: Even in the midst of our storms when we are unaware of who we are, we must trust and know that God is there. *Matthew 28:20 (NIV) states, "And teaching them to obey everything I have commanded you. And surely, I am with you always, to the very end of the age."*

CHAPTER 3: HAPPILY EVER AFTER; GOD CALLED YOU WOMAN

How do you know when you have met your ever after? Will it be the way someone looks at you or how just seeing someone makes you feel? In order to find your ever after you must do a meet and greet with yourself first. Yes, you have to find the woman God called you to be. Women should allow their minds to captivate instead of their bodies as this brings out her inner beauty. Scripture says, *"Your beauty should not consist of outward things like elaborate hairstyles and the wearing of gold ornaments or fine clothes. Instead, it should consist of what is inside the heart with the imperishable quality of a gentle and quiet spirit, which is very valuable in God's eyes", 1Peter 3:3-4 (HCSB).* So, in addition to this, if we think about it, the outward adornment will not carry us into an old age relationship because the outward appearance changes. Likewise, it is very important to invest in your inner being, so it captures your prospective suitor. What I do believe though, is when we wait on God, He will send us who He has for us, but first, we must find ourselves. How can you separate yourself from what you don't know unless you find you first? Are you willing to find you in order to find true love? Love found me when I least expected it. It was almost an instant connection, and it almost blindsided me, as well. Instant for me did not mean love, though, because God was in the midst of the union. Ultimately, when God has His hands on something, that's the instant I am speaking of because He allows you to feel something in your heart. He also will give you the room you need, and the space for your growth.

That being said, it was necessary to find me first; the woman God called me to be had to become visible to herself. It is impossible to find you while holding on to something or someone that does not belong to you. I found this out first-hand while in the relationship that almost took my life. That person was never meant for me. Although beautiful children were created from it, the time invested should have never been. So, I wanted to see the person that was seen from the eyes that found me attractive. Since I was a hurt individual from a previous relationship, I didn't want to bring that person forward in any way. In fact, after all I had gone through, I was ready to be by myself, and not invest in any other relationship for a while. It was an absolute must to transition into my new season with God's help. According to *James 1:17-19 (KJB)*, it says *"Every good gift and every perfect gift is from above, and cometh down from the Father of lights, with whom is no variableness, neither shadow of turning."* This scripture tells me that when God created me, He created me perfectly, so I am a good and perfect gift to anyone that receives me.

So, how did life get so messed up? How did I become a battered woman? What I now know is what held me captive back then, had to go. Because God gave us free will, bad decisions will be made *(1 Corinthians 10:23)*. It is those decisions that brought us harm. *You see,* fear had controlled my territory for far too long, and the beast inside me wanted to emerge, but I had to learn to keep it submerged in order for me to prevail. Anger and resentment will not be a part of who I'd become as it keeps me in my past. Women are powerful in their own right and hold the key to every single human life born on this earth so that makes us powerful at best. Our bodies transform in such a way that is powerful and makes us superhuman, so to speak. Our bodies are so full of life as it carries life and brings it into the world. Our success in being who we are is because of who God called us to be. Yet, people try to control us.

Women should rise above all adversity because we can introduce ourselves as someone that can bring change. Our very creation is a delicate piece of God's work. Even man could not see the creation of a woman according to the bible because he was put to sleep during our creation, *Genesis 2:22 (NIV)*. So as Adam was put to sleep, he had no knowledge of God's secret meeting with woman. An assignment was given to us during our development from Adam's rib, and when he awoke, there was no knowledge of our connection from the beginning until God introduced us. Scripture says "...He brought her to man", *Genesis 2:22 (NIV)*. Yes, we were even introduced in a special way. I am sure he was amazed by her beauty as well as her image in terms of how her body looked. The curves she possesses is God's masterpiece. So, the secret started with us and God and remains there today. Everything that goes on inside of our bodies when we bear children is God's glory. We were protected at that very moment from man. Therefore, even though we were taken from the rib of man, we came in a special way. Think about it; God didn't even create Jesus the same way He created Adam because through a woman He came. God decided, at that time, that women would have a special connection to life. Women are the secret place without knowing it was hidden inside man, scripture says *"The bone of his bones"* according to *Genesis 2:23 (NIV)*. Everything about our being is delicate and fragile. We actually lay down our lives to give life because we have no control during that time. Many have given their lives for lives to survive. We are sensational women given authority here on earth to produce and birth life into existence, and without us, through the work of God, it can't be done.

Therefore, once I transitioned into the woman I am today, I understood that God still saw me as the perfect image He created, but I am the one that stained the physical image by the life I chose, thereby, altering my assignment. It's time to decide that your broken past is not the image that will control your destiny. It's important to bear the fruit of God and to let His light shine above all things. So, although I had dreams of someone that would treat me like a princess and would value everything about me, I did not feel like connecting to anyone else at the time because they had to see me as God saw me first.

Also, God does not abuse in any way, so anyone that presents themselves that way, is not of God, and couldn't be for me. With this in mind, I prepared myself to just love myself where I was in my life and be perfectly fine with that. Over the course of years, and seeing how difficult relationships could be, it should not take much to not place yourself into another toxic relationship, or any relationship for that matter, that didn't place value on you. In doing so, you must be able to distinguish between the good, bad, and the ugly by allowing yourself time to adjust. I recall the dating process and being able to weed out everything that I would not allow in my life. If anything, compared to what I went through, in what I call my previous life, presented itself in any way, it would be an instant "no" for me. Setting your goals high and putting standards in place in terms of relationships is not out of the question. We, as women, should be able to feel bold, beautiful, and expensive all at the same time. Yep, just as expensive as each human life we, as women, give birth to. Our happiness and value are what make our ever-after even possible. When my divorce was final, I was able to appreciate all of myself. I had to set boundaries and put standards in place that would be realistic. When standards are not put in place from the beginning, then you could go right back into another toxic relationship because toxicity does not present itself early. However, watch out for that honeymoon phase, though, because each new relationship has them, so don't become distracted. Always keep your guard up because the enemy is sneaky.

Let's go back a bit. Think about the deception that Eve experienced in the Garden of Eden, *Genesis 3 (NIV)*. In paraphrasing, she was able to be deceived by something she saw as beautiful; something as simple as fruit. She was tempted by the devil. She looked beyond the bigger picture of the garden she was placed in which had everything Eve ever needed. She gave up *all* that God gave her for a small piece of fruit. We still do that today because we will turn around and accept the one thing that can harm us. However, there is something in the pit of your gut that says it's wrong, but we will ignore it while allowing someone to talk us into something that is no good for us. This should tell you that everything that looks good or better is not good for you. Temptation can be a very dangerous thing in any form; so, stay alert. Eve allowed Satan to deceive her with a piece of fruit that she was already forbidden to eat so just think about that for a minute. A piece of fruit is that all that your life is worth? Eye candy is what we call it today and both are used as an abstract in terms of what catches our eyes. According to www.researchgate.net (Symbolism of biblical forbidden fruit-ResearchGate) it states, "Forbidden fruit symbolizes a lie. Lies are usually very sweet but toxic to the human mind. Truth, on the other hand, can be very bitter, but it is always liberating." Forbidden fruit is used as an abstract, but it is so very real because many of us allow beauty to catch our eye at first glance. So, we must keep our eyes and ears open to be able to discern between the two, beauty as well as evil.

When I remarried, he was definitely a piece of fruit. Yes, that eye candy was so very pleasing to the eyes, but I could not take just his looks at face value. The character of a person is just as important. It is important to take your time and learn what's on the inside of the cover. This also shows us that what is offered to us in the physical at times is not always good for us because of the hidden agendas within it. Although he captured my eyes immediately, would he capture my soul? I had to figure it out by taking my time to know what was inside the wrapper, so to speak. It's like a piece of candy hidden in a package, but you can't determine its taste until you unwrap it in order to go through the process of tasting it. It does not matter the name on the wrapper, but it's important to see if it will keep its flavor over time. Keep in mind that everyone does not have the same taste buds, and what I like, you might not. So, will you allow yourself to just take any piece of fruit with the outside still on it without peeling back the layers covering the inside? I use fruit and candy as a metaphor to help you understand what is inside the heart of man. Eve's decision caused the fall of man by the one choice she made, and she gave man a taste. What she ate was pleasing to the eye, she was tempted, and that caused destruction for her soul; thereby, inviting the entire world to fall with her. A woman's choice is powerful, and at the very moment she takes her mind off of her heart and lets her mind take control, something disastrous could happen. Our minds can play tricks on us; so, monitor your thoughts about everything because it can be deceiving, but our hearts show our true character, I believe, so it's important to take your time.

Therefore, it is imperative for us to allow our hearts to guide us instead of our minds. That is where sin can start to live and manifest in a negative way. It takes time for our hearts to adjust in order to love something or someone. I honestly don't believe in love at first sight; instead, it's lust at first sight because we see first with our eyes and start to want the very thing that we call attractive but might bring harm to us. Webster describes lust as a "very strong sexual desire." *1 John 2:16-17 (KJV) says, "For all that is in the world, the lust of the flesh, and the lust of the eyes, and the pride of life, is not of the Father, but is of the world."* A sexual desire should not be the start of a relationship because it's about the physical connection. What occurs if this happens? Yep, a sexual relationship. During sex, bodily fluids are exchanged, the mind gets involved, and at that moment a connection is made that can change your life forever. So, in essence it's not about the whole person they desire, but only the temporary satisfaction that can lead to disappointment from those seeking a genuine relationship. Don't allow the sins of the world to cause you to fall into what is called a honeymoon phase that will fade once the newness has worn off because no relationship was formed.

Therefore, if we follow our hearts, that is what will bring us to our ever after, and we can live happily ever after in any situation that proves to be from love instead of lust. Our hearts would be in a better place also if we first prove to ourselves that we are worthy of ourselves. So, don't just give yourself away; protect your wholeness. Then anything that connects to us after that would be good because we have chosen to be in a place of wholeness which puts us in a great place with our mind, body, spirit and soul. The end result of Eve's downfall was her lust while being tempted which was temporary in comparison to what God has for us. Keep in mind that one woman brought death to an entire world. Although a woman's path was changed because of Eve, we now suffer pain through childbirth, but through God's forgiveness of sin, *Colossians 3:13 (NIV)* we remain His secret place. So, don't be fooled by temptation, but wait patiently on your completeness and allow your mind to be strengthened by it. Also, find forgiveness in your heart when you stumble, because you will, but just know that you can get back up.

Reflection: Forgiveness is essential to life thereafter. It's an opportunity for us to dig deep within our innermost beings in order to be entirely happy with oneself. *Matthew 6:14 (NIV) says, "For if you forgive other people when they sin against you, your heavenly Father will also forgive you."*

Daisy Arness Marrs

CHAPTER 4: KNOW YOUR WORTH; COME OUT OF HIDING

I had to learn to make myself a priority. Balance myself out in such a way in order to put my best foot forward. I learned to channel life differently to carry God's light within me in order to get to a better place. Therefore, we have to learn to keep our cups full, instead of half full, until they are more than overflowing with honey. Overcoming the challenges of life that we fear is an absolute must. Keeping yourself centered outside the hidden spaces of stress will help guide your heart. This will also aid in unnecessary trauma from the outside. I am not okay if I put everything or everyone else above me.

One of the hardest things that I had to learn was to not carry someone else's voice in my head because that is a heavy burden to carry. You are literally hiding almost everything about yourself when you do. Think about it! Most of the thoughts we have come from someone else. Either we channel what we hear on television, soak up what social media has to say, or digest what someone told us or said about us. Either way, hiding who we are is not acceptable. *Matthew 11:28 (NIV) says, "Come to me, all you who are weary and burdened, and I will give you rest."* This tells me the weight of the world will be heavy and hiding from it won't give us what we need if we are hidden within ourselves. In order to come out of hiding, we must replenish all that we gave up in order to know that we are worthy. Resting in the Lord will come easier when we do this. The protective shelter that we women once hid under can now be removed. So, we don't turn around and downgrade our worth as a woman at that moment by not prioritizing ourselves, we must rise above. You have to put yourself in a position to not allow others to cast doubts on your priority. So, don't let anyone lessen your worth. If we are hidden, all that we can gain will never be found. Likewise, all those negative conversations that will be thrown at you are not your burdens to carry. So, take them all to the alter, and leave them there.

Upgrading our thoughts makes us stronger individuals as we notice other people's energy not having any effect on us. I learned that the more that I connected to the word of God, the more sensitive I became to negative energy. It is time to choose your own thoughts so they can manifest your own awareness. Conversations with others that require us to be quiet and not have an opinion are like watered-down information that flows in one direction. It takes two people to have a conversation and a woman's voice is worth everything that is added to it. It simply would have no value if you had no opinion. We are worth every bit of weight that life can hold. When we come out from hiding from the voices that have told us that we can't do it, our light will shine brightly. We should also be courageous enough to stand against the principalities of darkness that try to count us out when we are seen while trusting what God has given to us.

The world does not understand the power we have when we stand under one voice. Coming out of hiding should help us recognize our true selves. Our opinions matter more than we realize. It is our time to take ownership of who we are. Even though we are individual women, together we are a revolution, and that makes us fierce. It is imperative that we create and write our own stories.

Many chapters of my own life became exposed because my ex-husband treated me as if I had no worth. I started to rewrite each chapter to be read differently as if the lines on each page existed for only one reason, and that was to meet every part of me that showed up. When deciding to share the sensitive part of you, consider what things you should keep private from others because what's unshared will forever be your secret places. What value do you place on yourself? Do you even know?

Now that my divorce was final, and I survived my courtroom experience, it was time for me to accept my new normal. I was able to get in my car after leaving the courthouse and drive to the voice on the other end of the phone. Yes, there was a voice that held me down, and carried me to that day. A voice that hid in the shadows. I was given an opportunity to reflect on the horrible details of my life. When leaving the courthouse, I did not focus on my ex-husband waiting for me, but on the powerful woman, I became. Notice I said, ex-husband. The sun felt brighter on my skin as it was shining ever so brightly just for me that day. It was as if God Himself was holding me saying, "I told you I got you." I was intrigued by how I was feeling. I felt as though I stood taller than the trees because that's how much freedom meant to me. It was an overwhelming feeling of gratitude, and honestly, it was about me for the first time in my life. I could definitely, "see clearly," as the old saying goes. I got into my car, turned on the ignition, and as music filled my car, I couldn't do anything but cry. I had to take a moment before driving off as I cried, because now, I understood the real feeling of freedom, and found it hard to wrap my head around it. I then found myself smiling more and feeling free to do whatever my heart desired. Life can be cruel in so many ways, and how we deal with the cruelness could be how we manage the rest of our lives.

After leaving an abusive relationship, I was determined to figure out who I was, what I wanted, and what I had learned throughout my life. I learned that I was the only one that was giving away my power to others who really had no meaning in my life. I was the "be there for everybody else person." Everything outside myself was more important. It was time to give people permission to enter my space rather than them forcing their way in.

Giving someone permission to come into your space is more than just saying, "yes." It is your presence that has to be entered into. Since your present moment is all you have to offer, you should protect it at all costs. Stand bold on the word "*no*" because you are the only one empowered at that very moment to accept or reject anything negative. Saying "*no*" should be used like your life depended on it, and in many ways it does. Learn how to say *"no"* and not care how others view it.

Anyway, when I found true love, after years of abuse, I was the one that owned it. I was the only one that could move forward with it. I was the only one that would say, "yes." Once we, as women, realize that what we allow in our lives can make us or break us, we can be on an extraordinary journey to those around us. If we think about it, we have an awesome glow of brilliance that reflects who we are individually, and it's a glow that draws people to us. The people that try and enter our presence can either be for us or against us. The dictionary describes presence as "The state or fact of existing." Our very existence can either draw negativity or positivity to us; so, because of our presence, it's up to us to decide. Life itself may have taught you that we should have an abundance of people around us, such as family, friends, or even strangers. However, what we don't see immediately is the enemy that has staged his or herself as one of them. We often find that we trust people sooner than later and find ourselves hurt when we realize that they are no more than just the enemy. Learning that you are the only one empowered to let people into your life and allow them to stay there, is beyond just your imagination. Why? Because you are the only one that can give someone permission to be there. Therefore, protect your space, ladies. It is not always possible to stop someone from hurting you, but the length of time you allow them to continue, is solely up to you. Ask yourself this question; How do you value yourself? You must dig deep within yourself to answer that question. After all, years of frustration, insecurity, anger, and maybe not loving yourself have built up, and you have to learn to pick it all apart. Allow your heart to heal in times when you feel that it has been snatched out.

I found out love is an action word, and for love, it has to be proven in many ways. How can you know if someone is against your very being? What are the signs that you should look for? Being divorced brings new meaning that does not include sadness, but a new-found sense of happiness. I have since learned that I am worth more than every sacrifice that I went through. Hiding makes us stay in a place that receives worry and doubt. It also makes you worry about things that you previously let go. Every bit of you is worth seeing and accepting. Who you are is part of the package. When you have accepted all of yourself and realize that today is all that you have because none of us can live in tomorrow until it comes, everything about you will become easy to accept. Then, each of your tomorrows can become a place of change and an opportunity to create your best self. Each of us can also learn to appreciate ourselves and not feel as though we have to hide to cover up things we see as unacceptable about ourselves. This, in turn, will help us present ourselves to, basically, the opposing side. Being able to be happy with your whole self allows people to see us differently.

Reflection: We are more than enough created in the image of God. *Genesis 1:27, says "So God created man in his own image, in the image of God created him; male and female created he them."*

Lady's it's important to expose yourself rather than allowing someone else the opportunity to do it. This you will thank me for later, because most of your outside world has already been revealed. God sees us before anybody so allow his creation to be front and center.

Daisy Arness Marrs

CHAPTER 5: A WOMAN ACTIVATED; THE SOUL OF A WOMAN

There is a quote that says, "the eyes are the window to the soul," and if that's true, what does yours say? When you think about it, your emotions are centered in and around your eyes. The tears you cry, the happiness that beams from them when you smile, or even the fear that lies dormant can be seen when someone looks you straight in your eyes. What about those dark circles beneath them when you have had many lonely sleepless nights? According to *Matthew 6:22 (ESV) "The eye is the lamp of the body. So, if your eye is healthy, your whole body will be full of light."* Also, as a nurse, I have stared death in the eyes many times throughout my nursing career. As someone nears death, their eyes become glassy or sometimes the pupils may become fixed or unresponsive as they close them for the last time. So, let's just say that what we speak or don't speak, the eyes speak as well. The dictionary describes the soul as, "a person's moral or emotional nature or identity: *in the depths of her soul, she knew he would betray her,*" it says.

Since many of us find ourselves in similar situations, ladies, protect you at all costs because betrayal can come in many forms. If you have been wounded by a man, or someone, so deep that it hurt you to your soul, you can move on from it. "Can I love again?" is what many of us ask. The answer is, absolutely! Stay in harmony with your truth because it's all you have, but don't just settle. Your eyes can shine bright again, and the brilliant light will shine through.

I remember the first day I saw the man I am married to today and the attraction I had for him. However, I also remembered the promise I had made to myself to protect myself at all costs. So, because this was a new version of me, I showed up differently. I also realized that I am worth every part of me. So, if and when I would remarry, he would have to be God-sent. No, really! I am serious! He had to know the Lord, and not by word alone, but by deed as well. I decided that I would never ever be broken again because my soul depended on how I responded to situations. Therefore, every part of me had to be protected, and my inner being was a major part of that protection. You have to protect yourself even if your promise to yourself keeps you in your moment for a while.

Anyway, when I remarried, after years of abuse and manipulation, it was then that I decided to create my own narrative. It was a promise to myself that I would never allow anyone to treat me like I had been treated my entire life. It was important for me to know that I mattered, and to love myself enough not to be easily accessible to anyone. I found that I was very attracted to this man, and he was definitely built differently. How he spoke and the way he carried himself was much different than the men I was used to seeing in my circle, so to speak. He wasn't like the usual street guy, if that makes sense. In addition, I must say that he activated every part of my soul, and he was starting to energize my emotions as if a bright light had been turned on. Honey, when I tell you this man was gorgeous, and his eyes were beautiful, and the way he looked at me, especially when he took his glasses off…that is another story. Remember now, I am talking about his soul now because his eyes, they lit up. Something inside his eyes caught me, and still captivates me to this very day. He will remove his glasses, and when I call his name, he looks at me and it's as if the look pierces my soul. I tremble just thinking about it as it brings a warm smile to my face.

So, this is the type of man that I chose to have in my life moving forward. Women have to find a place where it would be okay to express themselves outwardly by accepting who they have become, and I felt that I could do life with him. It's good for us to be able to show every woman that we can let our decisions move us forward based on how we feel, if we do it correctly. We have to become bold about what we want and then go after it. Go after your peace, ladies, and allow it to serve as your guide. I manifested the man that I wanted from the dreams I had as a young girl; I knew the one that I had previously could not be who God had for me. Don't stray away from your dreams because I believe it's God speaking to us in some way. Scripture says, *"Before I formed you in the womb I knew you, and before you were born, I set you apart…" Jeremiah 1:5 (NIV)* This tells me that God had already chosen whom He had for me. He set me apart from abuse that captured a large part of my being. He set me apart from destruction that tore down my foundation. He set me apart for my purpose. Therefore, I was free to discover who and what was meant for me. Oftentimes, I would dream about how a man would treat me when I was a little girl, and it was like the fairy tales we see on television. Even fairy tales are someone's reality, right? When women aren't treated correctly, they will have dreams or thoughts of someone that would, as a way of escape. That was me as well. So, I was captivated by everything about this man.

Ladies, why can't we have exactly what we want? Women love so hard that we forget to receive in return. Therefore, once out of the abusive relationship, it was important to not place myself back into the same type of situation by analyzing what was before me. It became my goal to live a productive life so that I could maintain myself as a woman by allowing someone to add to my value, and not take from it. How is it that a man can tell you what he wants and what he is looking for, and we accept that at face value? What about what we want? It is necessary to know what you want and not alter it; do this by setting goals. Yep, as I stated in the previous book I wrote, *"Know your worth and fight for it."* We, as women, should be able to first understand ourselves, put in the atmosphere what we want, and move from there. In doing so, also realize that there is no perfect person and even the visions that you have of whomever you choose as a partner that will ultimately fit into your space, will have big shoes to fill.

I feel that there is also a new generation of women that won't allow a man to dictate their future because of the choices we make and where we are in our lives. Women are refreshed in terms of where we were many years ago. They see relationships that have failed, and like me, set up a to-do list when searching for a partner in life, if they choose to have one. It's like when making out a grocery list, but an expensive one. We should write down all that we need and then go pick out what we want on that list. However, if it doesn't fit who you are once you have what you picked out, it's okay to let it go. Place yourself in a judgement-free zone. So, instead of someone choosing you, stay focused on your list and be happy with that decision you made. Most men might be offended by this, but we are okay with that as well, because that particular man doesn't have to be the chosen one. That's why the soul of every woman has not only captured its own identity, but finds that it is okay to choose when, and how, we will let someone into our life because our emotional energy has changed.

Many of us have also mastered the skill of *reset*. It is an alternative to what the status quo is, of how women choose to have a family, for example, and like the art and skill of mastering and molding your own craft, women now have a choice. I believe we have been hurt, and or manipulated, into relationships so much that we now choose to dictate our own lives. We can also now write our own tickets to a destination into our futures without the least bit of worry about how others feel. Women are no longer creatures of habit and are no longer predictable. Once our souls have been damaged, for example, we are able to reshape our course in order to have a different outcome, and then feel, "it is well within my soul," as they say.

Once I left the abusive relationship, I vowed to myself that I would have the man of my dreams in my life once I started dating again. Indeed, I have become that woman. The one that will have what she wants in a relationship and make no apologies for it. However, what this tells us is that there are people out there that want the same things. So, once I figured out who that was, there was no turning back. We can pick and choose someone that will love us the way we are supposed to be loved by taking our time and investing in the research. Men do this as well, because some have been hurt in such a way that they will look for someone that will add value to them as well as fit into their lifestyle. Therefore, since I felt like I was broken deep in my inner being for so many years, I promised myself that no one will be allowed to fit in that space ever again, that didn't add to, or live up to, my standards. There was a time in my life that I felt like I was damaged goods, and that I would not be able to find someone who would accept me where I was. It takes a lot for someone to take in someone else's brokenness and mold it into a beautiful piece of art. However, since so many people in the world felt like I did, it was an opportunity to reshape where I came from, and not let that create a narrative for who I was to become. It took time for me to reshape the moment when abuse both physically and mentally tried to change who I'd become. Years of brokenness tried hard to control how I showed up; it felt like it almost succeeded, but

I found my turning point.

Once I shared where I came from in life with someone I met, they could either accept or reject me, but I will not be judged. Becoming accountable for every situation in the past, helped me evolve as a strong independent woman. It was important to accept that my past was my past, and it was something I could not change. Don't allow anyone, ladies, to hold your past against you. I have since learned that some men are intimidated by strong independent women. But they will never understand a woman's point of view who has survived death only to rise up on the other side of it. We also can't waste our energy on things that we can't control, but the things we can change, immediately, we must.

Don't allow someone to leave you alone in your pain. The realization that we have come out with wounds from our past lives that have beat us down, leaving us bruised and some with permanent marks, will cause an awakening like never before. It is then we gain our independence to stand up for ourselves; by learning how to heal the wounds, by working on ourselves to be able to remove what caused the deepest pain that lies within our souls. Until then, we will manifest our dreams in a way that would be fulfilling to our hearts, and only then, can we give that part away. The transition into becoming who we really want to be as a woman will help us be the best version of us that we can possibly be. I found the man that activated the best part of me. In fact, he was looking for me as well, the part of me that is beautiful, strong, bold, and independent; the one that found herself in spite of it all. He needed a woman like me as we complement each other very well, but not only that, there is a deep God connection between us. It is so important not to stray away from your dreams, ladies, as they can be activated at a time that is least expected.

Reflection: Women have always been strong, but our might may have been weakened during a small moment in time. If we find the key to unlock the mystery behind the door that was closed on us, then everything waiting on the other side will fit. The soul of every woman depends on it. *Psalm 143:8 (NKJV) says, "Cause me to hear they lovingkindness in the morning; for in thee do I trust: cause me to know the way wherein I should walk; for I lift up my soul unto thee."*

CHAPTER 6: A SEAT AT THE TABLE

How often do you find that you have been a voice for many? So many women that have been pushed aside or have solely been forgotten about, have lost their voice. Oftentimes we feel as though a chair has been pulled from under us when, in fact, we were never asked to be seated. If you are honest with yourself, you probably were part of the forgotten. Each of us has been given our individual stories to go about life as we choose, but the damage was already done when we allowed someone else to choose for us. Somehow, as you prepared to have a seat at the table that you thought you were prepared for, you realized it's specifically for grown folks. You then realize you were not doing grown folk stuff at all. Instead, you were leisurely going about your life as if you had all the time in the world to get yourself together. In actuality, you were being exposed at this time, during your transition called life. It's hard to reposition yourself from things you don't know about. Therefore, once you allow yourself to transcend in growth, the transition then becomes easier.

However, there is a lot to unravel while you are trying to find your way. You may have become stuck because of the traumas you have experienced, or you didn't learn how to work through them. What do you do? You proceed with caution and you get stuck in transition. Hey, it's okay because most of us have been there. We must understand that there are conversations that need to be had that will help us get to the end of that unprotected space that nobody wants to claim. We must advance in our knowledge of things we are unsure of and find it safe to go after it. Since knowledge is power, as they say, let's just let wisdom become what we seek. Wisdom will play a huge part in our experiences that catch us off guard and alter our lives. You will find that it will be your closest friend. According to *Proverbs 3:13 (KJV), it states, "Happy is the man that findeth wisdom and the man that getteth understanding."* This scripture tells me that I should become wise about everything, and I should hold it close. I can't let what I don't know stop me from trying to invest in my mind though. So, if this is true, how did my life get so out of hand? It is very simple! The choices that others made for me in my youth, and the choices I made from my teenage years to adulthood, helped change God's plans in my life. Simply put, there was no wisdom there because I didn't seek it. I lost many opportunities while standing on someone else's foundation. Our own choices are what help create our stories, right? We can alter our purpose, but we can also get back on track when we understand where we should be. What happens though when something outside our power takes us on a path that, in so many ways, is meant to destroy us? Something that is so unthinkable and unbearable that it changes our life's course. Something that you have tried so hard to protect, only to lose it in a blink of an eye. Women are supposed to be strong no matter what we go through, but we are vulnerable in so many ways. Even Jesus's earthly mother, at her darkest moment, had to find her strength as a woman. I'm sure that the death of Jesus broke her down in many unimaginable ways, as she was present for His death *Matthew 27:55-56 (NIV)*. So, how did she endure such pain? Many of us have experienced that same pain, and we can't explain to you how to get through it. So, what is our biggest weakness, and when do we feel that the table that we prepared no longer has a seat for what we created? How do we shift the seats at the table to fit differently? Our children are, of course, our biggest weakness. They are also our greatest accomplishment. There are so many strong women that have had to carry the same burden as Mary. Although this does not exclude how a man feels, ours is different, because emotionally we are built differently.

Why did God choose for Jesus to be born through a woman without an earthly father connection? (Matthew, chapter one). Is there a teaching moment at the cross for us women? I have the pleasure of knowing a strong woman that shows up every day with strength, and she happens to wear a uniform. The badge, on the left side of her chest, that she attaches to the shirt she wears while on duty, did not separate her from the pain that many endure. Yet, there she stood very well groomed and professional. Even though I've heard her story before, this time would be different. She was scheduled to speak at an event that my organization put on for the community. Embracing a book she had written and wearing a crisp, white, spotless uniform shirt, and neatly pressed uniform pants, she stood before a crowd. While in uniform, her stance was different. Let me just say, she did not look like what she had been through. Is this the teaching-cross moment? She continues to show up as if nothing tragic had happened to her while helping others through possibly the same fate. To have to walk with honor when so much trauma had almost knocked her out only for her to rise above with a smile with the help of the Lord. I saw a beautiful, strong, black woman in that moment. A woman with courage and clout. A vulnerable woman in a moment of power that did not lose who she was. A woman that ultimately gave her pain to God to carry. Scripture tells us that God will never leave us nor forsake us, *Deuteronomy 31:6 (NIV)*. But, although for a short while, we may feel separated from Him; He never leaves us, according to His word.

Someone so precious to her was no longer in earthly form. She started to question God, but as she stated in her writing, *"God then spoke back to me plain as day and said, Dear Child, I lost my only begotten son too, so I feel your pain."* Is this the teaching-cross moment? Are women supposed to learn from Mary? It's like Jesus, when His earthly life was over, calling Mary "woman", *John 2:4 (NIV)* instead of "mother" while on the cross as He was about to give up the ghost and return to His Heavenly Father, *Matthew 27:50 (NIV)*. Jesus was separated from God while here on earth although protected, but not on the cross, *Mark 15:33-34 (NIV)* and separated from His earthly mother when returning to His Heavenly Father. Is this our teaching-cross moment? What does a woman represent at the cross? How do you pick yourself up if you don't know His voice? How can you feel his presence in your time of need? The very thing that should have taken the life out of this woman, because part of her is no longer here, didn't. Instead, she says that *"the trauma she experienced wasn't her fault, but healing was her responsibility."* That very woman is Indiana's own Southport Assistant Police Chief, Lossie Davis, and not only did she trust in God, but she also didn't allow herself to be lost in her pain too long. Her very weakness became her strength as she allowed God to help find the purpose for her pain. I felt her strength through her words while embracing every part of what she was saying. Quietly, while listening, I became her. I know that pain and I have shed those tears. The strong woman that must continue life without a life that she created, is wisdom. Only a wise woman can move past the unknowing, but it is the unknowing that she must move beyond.

Ultimately, we must realize, as painful as it can be, we must move forward. It is important to find the strength to pull you through the tough times even while shedding tears. Ask yourself if you can sit in seats that bear that same kind of pain? How can you move beyond the table? Can you lose and gain at the same time? I know her pain all too well because I too have an empty seat. We, like Mary, lost our earthly child, but knowing that they are resting in the Lord gives us comfort. That is, indeed, a seat that no mother wants to take. One that had to be reshaped in order to survive while realizing you can't do it alone. Although life shows up in many ways to counter punch what God has for us, we must be prepared to stand. So, not only can we walk out of purpose, but others will also painfully alter it for us, and it won't matter how and when it occurs, because our pain will still run deep.

Also, when we decide to go outside of our purpose and attach ourselves to someone that hurt us, we form our own path, and that, my friend, was the beginning of multiple chairs being pulled from under me. Yes, this is a different kind of strength as well, because there are different kinds of losses. A path that almost destroyed me, and the future that I was provided, was redirected. Therefore, our many tables are attached to who we then become in the moment. We can become displaced and mismanaged if we are not focused. We have to learn to accept ourselves for who we are in all of our circumstances, good or bad. I say this because we may find ourselves at a disadvantage if we choose not to walk in love no matter what. We, in fact, should never let what happened to us keep us in an unforgiven state because this also plays a specific part in where we sit. If we dismiss what happened in unforgiveness, we can't heal through it.

Therefore, we have to grieve through it in order to help others out of it. We are who God created us to be individually by collectively standing in one accord. Each and every one of us has a role to play and how we show up determines our course in life. God provided not only me a seat at His table, but you as well. Like for Lossie, and for many of us, life changed drastically; but once we discover God's purpose, life becomes a little easier. Because of this, we have many opportunities in picking the table at which we choose to sit. Who will you invite to yours? Will your enemy be invited? Not many of us really think about the consequences of inviting the wrong people into our space though. It may take you awhile to shift your mind from yesterday, but you can do it while not ever forgetting, but by thinking about it differently.

God will find purpose for your pain. How you show up is up to you. Speak through it and teach yourself healing if you must, but whatever you do, heal. Trauma, as we learned, comes in many forms, but God is always there ready to hold us through it. Maturing into God's word is a lesson that I learned while going through, but once on the other side, I felt He was always there. I also decided that my life circumstances would make room for me, and my confidence would help me advance while helping others.

Learning to own your transition into greater, will also become an opportunity for growth. There were many times that I did not feel worthy enough to be around others that may have been more advanced in life than me but putting myself down was no longer an option. When you realize that you are valuable, then your voice can no longer be silenced. All the opportunities that passed you by are suddenly right before you. Your voice is your microphone, so use it wisely. Women are so often taken for granted that they lose their own value by thinking negatively. Sharpening your mind increases the possibility for you to trust yourself by owning your own ability to shine. When you put your best foot forward, it is then that you see that you have made an impact on others, and a sisterhood can then be established. As you begin to put your heart and soul into everything you do, you can make a difference in society.

This is the time when you learn that the seat that you were seeking was your own. Yes, you own each and every one of them. The table then shifts into parallels that have been equal to what you knew all along. You have always been great; it was just the way you viewed yourself while going through. It wasn't until you got out of your own way that everything started to flow in sync with God's word. What should we have learned when we got up from the table though? Ultimately, once I was given a seat, I learned so much from all the disparities in my life. When given an opportunity to do life again, take it by moving from where you are, and learn from your mistakes, but don't repeat them. It's good to move past what caused you pain as long as you grow with it. Love your good memories while giving your bad ones to God.

Don't allow others to keep you anywhere against your will, no matter what, and that includes in your past, unless it is for your good and for instructional purposes only. But you have to be the one to re-spin it to fit where you are today. If God will not remember them, why should you let others. Don't allow the one that broke you to keep you there. God gave me a seat at His table, and by listening, I learned that many will not have the opportunity that I have. Why? Because many will not pay attention to their mistakes and will not find the appropriate conversations that bring change. Let this be your *Ted Talk* moment. Always position yourself to sit at the head of the table, and don't allow anyone to tilt it. When you choose to stay where you are in life, it will, indeed, pass you by. All of the lessons you should learn when seated should give you enough information to change course.

However, it requires a lot of study time to examine your mistakes. Not the type of studying you think, but actually studying life yourself. All the material that will be laid out before you should be enough for you to pass or fail. Paying attention to each and every word written will help you through life. The words will be written on your heart and give you clear instructions. When you stray away from what is provided to you, then negative things may come your way. Also, pay attention to the instructions laid before you so you can maneuver through life as gently as possible. How is it that we can be given specific instructions and not follow them? Whether it comes from your parents, your doctor, or a teacher, pay attention. God also speaks to us and gives us specific instructions through His word. Once information is given to you in order not to mess something up, take it. Listen to those who are wise because they have either lived it, been taught it, or studied it to perfection. You should become wise in all that you have done or will seek out to do. Wisdom is worth every bit of the instruction received. Scripture says, *"Do not forsake wisdom, and she will protect you; love her, and she will watch over you. Wisdom is supreme; therefore, get wisdom. Though it cost all you have, get understanding." Proverbs 4:6-7, (NIV).* Why is it that this scripture calls wisdom, "her"?

Could it be because women seek answers, or we dig deeper to find the right answer? We seek to nurture things as we help them develop. We are the first to protect as we shield our children even while in the womb. We are definitely the first line of defense. You cannot get to our child unless you go through us first. We understand the assignment. Although we bear the burden of that pain when that child is lost, our strength must carry us through. Our courage is our shield because even though we may hide behind it, we must prevail. We will protect our homes just as our bodies protect our babies. Our entire bodies weep when we can't protect our child. We are the *secret place* that provides life, as stated in the previous chapter.

Learn everything about wisdom while seated at the table because it will grow old with you. Growth only comes from wisdom because the more you learn, the more you know. You could then teach others to master their skill of knowledge. Learn from a woman's strength and pain because you can't have one without the other. One of the worst pains a woman can feel is during childbirth, yet she can't remember it, and each birthing pain will be different. So, it's possible to just put all that you have gone through in the back of your mind and seal it there. Grab hold to the light that God provides and let that outshine your darkest moments. He will provide you comfort at His table and every seat you take from then on will become easier. There is also shelter at His table as His protection will guide you. Let every part of you be protected like you protect the life you carry as your natural instincts kick in. Pull from all the instructions He has provided you secretly, so you can outwardly show the wisdom you gained while understanding that every seat taken from now on will be one that you provide.

Reflection: Everyone is not offered a seat at the table, so when you are, do sit wisely. Bring with you the most important part of you, and don't conceal your identity. Don't become like Judas and be deceitful in your taking as it will only lead to disappointment. *Luke 22:14 (NLT) "When the time came, Jesus and the apostles sat down together at the table."*

Daisy Arness Marrs

CHAPTER 7: STAY IN YOUR NOW; LOVE DEPENDS ON IT

When *true* love finds you, never let it go. Love can present itself in many ways, but there is a type of love that we should look for. What is love you ask? Webster dictionary describes love as an intense feeling of deep affection. I have come to understand that there is a difference between love and true love. It is also described as a strong and lasting affection between spouses or lovers who are in a happy, passionate, and fulfilling relationship. This says a mouth full because I'm sure many of us that have been in a relationship have felt all of this at one point. Love, if you are not looking for it, can catch you off-guard. In addition, you have to recognize the difference between someone wanting you rather than them valuing who you are. This, my friend, is a special kind of love. Look at it this way; when someone wants you, they are actually looking at the physical part of you, the lust of you, the part that gets their hormones raging, and the part that they can easily walk away from because they actually got what they came after. But, if someone values you, they want every part of who you are and will be willing to invest in you, nurture you, and truly love you, mind, body and soul.

So, now that you know the difference, how will you proceed forward with relationships? Will you be drawn into someone else's physical attraction of you? Further, when you have found your happy place, it will become important to stay in your "now" because it will depend on how you feel right now; how you control your own emotions. I recall the goosebumps, and the way I felt when I was with him. As time went on, the compassion we showed and had for one another grew intense as we found ourselves not wanting to be without each other. This is what I still feel today with my husband. It's an emotion that I never thought I would feel because it's not just a physical attraction, but an emotional one as well.

Is this what love feels like? Yes, it is a love that is unconditional. This is a soul connection, ladies. Can I even get past the pain of my previous relationship? These are expected questions, especially for me. Well, the answer to this question is a profound, "yes." I would think of this question often when in his presence at the beginning. He was my dream come true standing right in front of me. Although, I had nothing to compare it to, he made me feel loved; mind, body and soul. A love that would shield me from all sides moving forward. The love that said I could trust again. An overwhelming feeling of wanting me is what he made me feel, as well. Prior to him, my life consisted of loneliness, pain, and separation because I did not feel I belonged. How was I supposed to know if what my body was feeling was love or not love at all? How could I tell it apart? After all, as stated above, people can show up in such a way that can make you see or feel something that could later turn out to be a disaster.

I am remembering the little girl, right now, that loved her father and needed him. However, I still never felt like this before, in terms of how to receive love in any form, but I embraced all of it. My father did not make me feel safe, but somehow that is what I was feeling now when in his arms. In addition, I was not made to feel protected, but that is what I was feeling in his arms. Feeling these emotions from a man as an adult is something I had never felt before. It made me feel the giddiness of a young girl and it made me want more.

I needed more, not to only escape from my past, but to not let it control the situation I came from by controlling the narrative. Because "now" is all I have. A feeling of euphoria when I was around him would have me on a natural high because he made me feel whole. Indeed, he would have my hormones raging by just the sight of him. He would intentionally come around when I was at work just to make my day better or call me just to hear my voice as my voice made him feel good, as well. It was not just a physical attraction between the two of us, but the intellect we both shared like a soul-to-soul connection. His eyes would beam at the very sight of me, and I needed all of that. I now know that he needed me as much as I needed him. Coincidentally, he still does this same thing today, and I would not have it any other way.

Life was starting to be amazing as I started to not let my past control my emotions, but I was also learning that I was safe in my now. It was finally about how I felt. My happiness was finally being valued by someone other than myself. Since God is love, according to, *1 John 4:16 (ESV)*, it is important for us to understand that our emotions can be front and center, and that eventually, we can find genuine true love because it does exist. The type of love that has you increasingly wanting more. Love, to me, is possibly one of the most important emotions we are to feel when dealing with human contact. Being able to understand how to connect my emotions to what I was feeling was a mystery to me because I was trying to recognize what I did not previously know existed. True love does exist, ladies, and it is not about making you feel like someone's possession. But it is about the burning passion you share between the two of you when you are not at your best. Without the makeup, and without the sexy clothes. You should be made to feel special in every aspect without exception.

My father did not show me how to receive or give love, so how was I able to understand what I felt or how to give it back? Ultimately, I learned to give back what I felt emotionally, and what I embraced had no boundaries. Embracing something that is foreign, required a little research though. Not the research you are thinking; I had to analyze each part of me in order to digest my feelings. It was time for me to get radical for myself by putting all of me into my emotional state.

I would often pull back because everything had to go my way in the relationship. I had to protect myself, my feelings, and now was the time to put me first. When you have promised yourself that if, and when, you get into another relationship, you would put yourself first, pulling back may become necessary. Taking your time and not playing with the thought of a new romance that would involve intimacy is something that you have to build upon. However, I found all that I was receiving very gratifying. Romance does not always have to involve sex, so don't let your emotions get you in trouble, but know it is okay to let go once you find your someone. He was romancing my mind as I had to learn to filter out what I previously thought love was. Taking the lead in the relationship helped me understand what I was getting myself into because I was on my time.

Everything about the new man in my life felt right. When I saw him for the first time, I felt butterflies in my stomach, and it still happens today. We are engulfed in each other's love wholeheartedly. Ultimately, the love that I needed depended on the human connection missing my entire life. I needed his touch, and I needed him near me. Every time we got together when dating, I was front and center, and he was very attentive. He would make sure to handle me softly and make every part of us getting together about me. In addition, he would also protect the delicate side of me by shielding my heart. My very soul depended on all he had to offer. It was the simple things that drew me closer to him. This was the man of my dreams and loving him was easy. After dating for a while, our love grew stronger, if that was even possible. I could not believe after the life that I had lived prior to meeting him, I would meet someone as wonderful as him;

although, I would not accept anything less.

Ultimately, I realized love was not something that you could speak of lightly because it must have action behind it, as well; it's actually much bigger than you or me. Love is definitely an action word. Since God is love and gave His one and only son, as stated in *John 3:16 (ESV)*, how can someone show their love for you in comparison? We understand that it is not possible, but knowing who God is, should be an attribute for which we look. When you find love, it should cover a variation of what scripture describes. Scripture says *"Love is patient and kind; love does not boast; it is not arrogant or rude. It does not insist on its own way; it is not irritable or resentful, it does not rejoice at wrongdoing, but it rejoices with the truth.", 1 Corinthians 13:4-8 (ESV)*.

Therefore, it does not only consist of what we say or how we say it, because actions, as we have heard, speak louder than words. After what I went through in my life, I needed love more than anything because it was absent in my life and actions are now a requirement. It is important to know that me loving myself first helped me to receive all that he had to give. There was no way anything I experienced was any form of love, and I do not care how often I heard it. Not knowing what it was, caused me to go through things that most people could never imagine. My own life story is, after all, like some type of movie, all wrapped up into one life. If you find yourself absent from love in your life, and you are in a serious relationship, you must separate from it. Do not just settle, ladies!

There were many tricks of the devil that showed up against me. So, when you find your person, it is important to be able to discern between the two. Because love can be masked differently, if not from God. It is possible to stay in your now by accepting what is going on within your life and understand that now is all that you have; so, choose wisely. Once you create your moments of importance, cherish them for a lifetime because love depends on it.

Reflection: True love can catch you by surprise and send you spiraling. It's great to create new memories as long as they are not sad ones. Invest in your now by doing your research on love so that your happiness stays in front of you. Make each day count, as if love does actually depend on it. *1 Corinthians 16;14 (ESV) says, "Let all that you do be done in love."*

Daisy Arness Marrs

CHAPTER 8: EMPOWERED AND BEYOND

Becoming empowered, to know that peace presents itself in silence, will help you walk away while gently saving yourself from all negativities. It is also an opportunity to gain your own personal empowerment by letting peace become part of your superpower. When we understand that peace is not loud, we can then move gently while grabbing hold of it. Peace is calming, gentle, relaxing, loving, trauma free, and intentional. It is not only something that you need, but that you should demand. Scripture says, *"And the peace of God which surpasses all understanding, will guard your hearts and minds in Christ Jesus." (Philippians 4:6 ESV).* This tells me that none of us know ahead of time that someone coming into our space will try to take away from us that which was given from God, but we can have it. We have the power to maintain it, so when anything other than peace shows itself, leave it. We must know that nothing is beyond our power when we put it in God's hands. We cannot be blindsided by the nonsense of others that get satisfaction from destroying someone's peace. The place where you lay your head down every single night should be your place of solitude. Indeed, it should be a place to lock out all that is going on in the world that could bring chaos into your life. Do not become blind to the maliciousness of others because your life depends on it.

How do you take control of your own life? It comes by achieving something on your own sometimes. Like when you have made the choice to put yourself first. Most women have removed themselves to make sure everyone else is good while we are somewhere in a corner soaking in loneliness. You must recognize your own power and make it intentional when it comes to you. When we are able to build up our self-esteem, and to do it with all the confidence in the world, it is then that we have moved beyond someone else's thoughts of us. Do not allow someone else's words control your thought on how you view yourself.

It is now time to breathe in strength and be ok with exhaling all the weakness that made you feel like you could not stand on your own. Being fragile when dealing with certain things was something that I had to take a serious look at because it was one of my weaknesses. Oftentimes, I wore my feelings on my sleeves not understanding the impact they may have on others. Actually, it was not until I wrote my first book that I realized that I was way more fragile than I could have ever imagined.

How is it that I learned so much about myself in my latter days? Well, it is called wisdom, and with wisdom comes growth. The Bible speaks of wisdom in *Proverbs 4:6-7 (NIV)*. It states, *"Do not forsake wisdom, and she will protect you, love her, and she will watch over you"*. The Bible also speaks of our latter days saying, *"Though your beginning was small, yet your latter end would increase abundantly" Job 8:7 (NKJV)*. Some may find wisdom sooner than others, while some may not find it at all, because they are not aware of what is going on in their lives. We must learn to master the craft of discernment in order to separate the destruction from others, immediately. So, when life throws you a curveball, and you think that you have caught it because it came directly at you at full speed, and you thought you could handle it, not realizing that what came at you, knocked you right off your feet intentionally. It is time to move out of your own way in order for your gift to show up. You now have figured out what it was and felt the impact of it full force.

Actually, here is what I learned during those difficult times. I learned that I am the best of me right now; because in my younger days, I stored so much of others inside me that I was almost destroyed. It is like people were layered on top of me, and I was buried deep down under them. It was hard to breathe, and I had to actually peel them off of me, mentally, one at a time.

Have you ever been given the opportunity to actually look back over your life and question your actions? This is the time you either get mad, happy, or find joy in what you remember. I call those "shedding moments" because you have been given an opportunity to reflect and reject. You can now shed off, layer by layer, everything or everyone that made you mad. Stand in your shower, for example, and metaphorically wash until you release and let go. Peel off the bully in your childhood, peel off the negativity thrown at you as a teenager, peel off the abuse that you went through as a young adult, peel off the teacher that said you cannot do it, and peel off anything that brought you pain in your life. Finally, when it is all said and done, peel off the rejection you felt all your life, and give it to God.

Now you can hold on to everything that brought you joy because those are the things that kept you here. That is why you are not in your grave today. Those things that brought you joy, and the people that stood ten toes down for you, are what kept your pulse at an even rate, your blood pressure down, and your heart from pounding profusely. Now do not get me wrong, we will continue to fight demons as long as we allow them to present themselves in our lives, instead of rebuking them.

In addition, scripture says in *1, Peter 5:8 (NIV)*, *"Be alert and of sober mind. Your enemy the devil prowls around like a roaring lion looking for someone to devour."* This statement alone tells us that for which to prepare. Yep, prepare for the unknown because the devil is always busy. We know that he does not present himself with horns, or a face like a wild beast, because that is fiction. In fact, he is dressed in your favorite Gucci suit or pulls up next to you at a stop light. Heck, he will even hold a door for you when entering a store. You will like this one. He will even sit next to you in church and say, "Amen," so do not let him catch you sleeping. What I am trying to say is that the devil is the everyday person that is trying to befriend you. Most of the time, I believe there are more wrong people than right ones that try to enter our life. Just think about it! How many people have you left behind in your life because of who they showed up as?

When I started to pay attention to my feelings and stopped really caring about how others saw me or felt about me, I felt better about myself because their actions showed me who they really were. My body stopped going through this spiral of emotions as I started to validate myself. I wrote in my previous book, "Know Your Worth and Fight for It." This quote still resonates with me deep in my soul. Why? Because that is when I realized I had found the best part of me. I am worthy of everything good, and I was not whole until I found myself. Everything about who I was came from knowing my worth. It is as if I took a scalpel and started examining myself layer by layer. There were so many mysteries about who I was. Although it took time to go layer by layer, it was worth all that I found. So, the introduction to self is finding a powerful human being that was beneath the pieces of me that were broken.

The devil always wants us to not think about ourselves, but about what he can give us. Remember when he kept trying to tempt Jesus. It was always what he could do for him, so he tried to tempt him more than once while he was in the wilderness by saying, if you do this, I will give you this. In *Matthew 4:1-11 (NIV)*, Jesus demonstrated that we could resist the devil along with all those fiery darts he throws at us, and he has no choice but to flee.

Learning that we are empowered to be bold, in terms of what we will and will not accept, is just the beginning of how good life could be. Let our *no* be *no* and let what we say broaden all the *yeses* that are coming our way. Women are being empowered each and every day as men try to take our worth from us. They think that we are a vessel that is weak, but God gave us our strength. We can be bold because every stance that we take as a woman strengthens our desire not only to be seen, but to be heard. Women are magnificent beings, strong and wise, and since we have decided to move beyond what broke us, we must capitalize on everything that helps us grow.

Reflection: Life is a journey, and we only get one. Become empowered to be who God created you to be. Put yourself at the very top of the list and do not hesitate to shut out anyone that opposes you. *1 Corinthians 16:14 (NIV)* says, *"Do everything in love."*

CHAPTER 9: SPEAKING TO MY YOUNGER SELF; MY FIRST LOVE

When we put trust in man, he will let you down every time. So, if we realize this from the start, it will save us a lot of heartbreak. Therefore, I realize now that I should have been the first person to embrace my love by first loving myself. I should have loved all of me before giving any of me away. I should have invested in all of myself by prioritizing everything about me. Which includes all my interests, thoughts, feelings, and desires. Yep, it is all about me. As what you want and do should be all about you. There are selfish reasons here because when you remove yourself from an equation, you do not exist because no one sees you. You limit your voice and shatter all your prospects. Once you realize that all of you is important, from birth to where you are today, life takes on a new meaning.

Think about it, we were made by our Creator, and we were made in His image, *Genesis 1:27 (NLT),* and all of those matters. So, this means that I am just as important as the next person. I received my official stamp of approval from my heavenly Father. So, I should have demanded respect for my person. There is no way I should have been a tormented little girl before the age of five, one that was very shy as well as an introvert without any direction. A little girl that did not feel loved by her father, someone that was supposed to be my first love, and was to embrace everything I was to become. Ultimately, he let the beginning of my life dictate my future.

In order to speak to my younger self, I must first remember where I came from, the obstacles that were in my way, and reimagine a time when life could have been different. I had to begin by loving myself first, and that required loving every part of me. First things first; I had to visually see myself back then in order to understand where I was, and then think about how it mentally affected me growing up. Things definitely should have been different for a young girl that never asked to be born in the first place.

When I look at myself in a picture as a little girl, I wonder what was going through my mind at the very moment the picture was taken. Was she ever told that she was loved and that she could do anything that her soul desired in life? What was my life like on any given day? Since many of my younger days were filled with sadness, as I remember when in the presence of my father, the pictures that I took actually captured my real happy moments as a little girl. I have a photo of myself with my family when I was around three or four years old. When I look at it, I feel sadness simply because of what I remember. My father was in the picture as well, sitting next to my mother with my older sister in front of him, as I sat, not smiling, on my mother's lap. Although I was well-groomed, there was sadness in my eyes that I felt when I sat back and stared at it. I do recall living as a family in the house that we were in when the picture was taken.

Why am I only concentrating on the negative though? I would like to feel that, although sadness dwells in my thoughts, there were a lot of happy times as well. What would I say to my younger self at this point in my life? As I concentrate on saying the right thing, I would say that God loves you and you were created for a purpose. You are simply more than enough. No one can ever take His love away from you. You are a beautiful little girl with so much potential. And I would instill the word of God into myself because when He created me, I was all that He thought of at that moment. This would be a moment to give me my gems because this is the age that development starts as we express our needs, feelings, and thoughts, according to "Very Well Family" (verywellfamily.com). During this time, I still loved my father though, and needed him without knowing it. Nothing that he had done to me felt wrong as a little girl.

My development, at this age, was not hindered because of how I was treated. In fact, I think I was above average at this age. As I advanced in age, life would continue to be sad at times in small pockets of my life. I would remember all that my mother had to go through as a single parent raising three little girls and say that she was our shield. I would remember that my father was a man that I looked up to no matter what he did wrong, and I would explain to myself that was not enough. I have learned that while my father was never connected to me emotionally, he was still my father. Although he should have been my first love, I did not learn how to love at all because there was no physical attachment there. Emotionally, I was starving and sought him to feed my soul. I needed his touch, and for him to wipe away my tears. I believe that we, as little girls, develop a false sense of security in someone else if we do not get what we need from our fathers as children. We should be placed in an environment that would provide love and nurturing as children, and that would help us understand life as we grow. We ultimately may look for it in someone else as we grow.

What would I tell my younger self at this point? Every part of you is worth the wait. You will show up as this beautiful girl that will live life on purpose. I would also tell myself that my strength and courage would carry me through. However, so many women are left alone to fight their own battles when it comes to figuring out life, with or without a man. This was a time when I should have learned how to advance into womanhood and feel extremely proud of myself. I should have also learned about the stages of life that teenage girls would eventually go through that may cause heartbreak, but instead, I accepted defeat. My father should have been the first man to hold my hand and say, "Everything is going to be alright." Additionally, I should have been able to enjoy all that life had to offer at a time in my life that was most meaningful. He should have also been my first date so I could have learned how to date. It was a time when my father should have been grooming me to know what it feels like to fall in love for the first time and then to have my heart broken. He should have been there to help me through it, but instead, he threw me to the wolves by not being there.

Now I was reflecting on how to move forward without any direction from a man. How do I compensate for what I missed? Although there were instances of happiness that I remember as a little girl when living with my father, there were not many because there was so much sadness, it overshadowed the good times. Why do we reflect so much on the negativity in our life? Why don't we spend the same energy on the good times as we do the bad times? When we do that, we are sending our bodies on a roller coaster of negative emotions by not honoring who we really are. If you knew your own identity and the weight that it carries, would you still be afraid? Did you know that in order for someone to bring you down to their level, you were at your lowest point in life? You will put yourself in a box not understanding that you have put a limit on yourself.

Anyway, while looking at the picture, it was as if I were speaking through it. Slight chills would come on me as I reminisced about the moment that photo was captured. My older sister was in the photo, as well as my father, my uncle, and my mother's friend. I smiled a little as I remembered me and my older sister playing in the yard of the house where the picture was taken. Then laughter came over me as I remembered the boys from next door playing with us through a fence. I can also see the coal-burning stove that we played with in the living room of the house. While playing, my older sister and I accidentally fell into the wood-burning stove while the wood was burning, and we were burned really bad on our arms. The screams we both let out were piercing because of the pain that we felt. I can also see our little arms blistering up quickly from the burns.

Now as I put the picture down, I look at my right elbow where the now healed scar remains. I smile even though at that moment I felt pain just remembering the shy little girl that adored my family. It makes me understand, as I look at the healed scar on my body, that we are also to heal mentally. Therefore, the scars we received in our past, can also help us heal as we can prevent the same mistakes from happening to us again.

But now, instead of pain, I feel joy as if I was playing with my sister. What was I doing? I was remembering myself in one of my vulnerable states but found joy in those moments. I allowed a new set of emotions to fill me up and set aside the sadness of my childhood as I reminisce on the moments that made me smile. During this moment, I am learning to accept myself at that age. I gave myself permission to accept how I saw myself in the world while living back then when my father was in control. I let go of how I was perceived by others and found myself through that picture.

Then I picked up another picture of when I was about nine or ten years old. I was tall and sort of skinny, but I remember that I used to be called fat in the sense that I was bigger than my sisters, and everyone always talked about my big behind which made me feel self-conscious about my body image. I started to think about many other things that were going on in my life through that moment in time. I made myself feel emotions about how it felt being called out of my name. I started thinking early about my body image and how others saw me based on the name-calling. Constantly hearing that I had a big behind made me feel self-conscious about it, so my journey of losing weight started early. In each photo I viewed, I was in Cadiz, Kentucky, my hometown. I found that to be fascinating.

I then started to think about that day and what that day could have been like for me. I was with my sisters, and cousins in the photo, and I remembered us playing in my grandmother's yard running up and down a hill. I again felt joy instead of sadness because through those photos I existed. God saw fit for me to be in that moment to enjoy everything that He is, and that is love.

Looking back over my life, what would I tell my younger self today? The first thing I would say is that you were loved. The nights that you felt all alone, you were loved. Love is what gives us power because we were created out of love; God's love. Tell your younger self that you are fantastic in everything that you do, and that everything about you makes room for you. There was no way I could have understood that as a child, but just stay in the moment and relax because God has got you. Take care of yourself with each age of remembrance. Play in the dirt longer and laugh a lot. Speak out for yourself more, and do not let someone else determine your worth. Oftentimes, that is when we feel betrayed by others, and our perspective about ourselves is taken over by man, the man we call, "dad." Learn to navigate through life's challenges without losing who you are along the way. Build confidence in yourself and do not feel powerless. Grab hold of your weaknesses to evolve into your wholeness. After all, many of those weaknesses I brought forth with me. Get to know every part of you, and take time in doing so. Do not become addicted to your past by allowing it to happen again. They say *time is of the essence,* so, take time in every twenty-four hours given to us to just *be.* This would have allowed me to separate my pain from growth, and to mature in a more promising way. Because every bit of pain that was thrown my way was meant to break me down. Every age is temporary, so find strength in each number gained.

When it comes to relationships, *wait!* Do not allow society to make you think that by a certain age you should be married and have children, and that your time is running out if you do not. There is a phrase that says *time is on your side* and I feel that this can be true in many ways. This says to me that if you adjust a situation to fit you in the allotted timeframe of your choosing, and stick to it, you will accomplish what you seek, and timely. Waiting would have allowed me to prevent all the wasted years by understanding that what I went through was a temporary situation that led to bad things. Put together a select committee within yourself to pluck out the bad parts while savoring the most flavored things about you. My body grew up before I was ready as my mind had not yet developed. My perspective on life back then was to fight through while not fighting for myself.

Lastly, know who God is; search for Him because then you would have known what true love felt like early on. This would have prevented me from accepting false narratives.

Now that I have said all of this, what would you tell your younger self? How can you dig deep within to find out who you would have wanted to be and actually get there without so many mishaps along the way? The most important thing to say to you is that you are forgiven; now move on. However, it is necessary to embrace the young *yous* that are growing up in the world without direction. The young girls that are lost and searching to find their way, but only held back from all the obstacles put before them. You must be able to reach one in order to teach one, as they say, so their younger selves can flourish in society today. Teach them to maximize themselves to advance in their growth. It is necessary to understand, that at any age, you matter.

Reflection: Always promote you so you won't be lost in the shuffle. Prioritize yourself while teaching selfcare. Don't ever minimize the child in you, but be sure to grow beyond your yesteryears. Always accept and love every part of you through each stage in life as you remind yourself that you are part of God's plan. *Jeremiah 29:11 (ESV) "For I know the plans I have for you," declares the Lord, "plans for your welfare and not evil, to give you a future and a hope."*

Daisy Arness Marrs

CHAPTER 10: THE UNDOING OF EVERY ATTACK

L earning that "misery loves company" is more than a popular saying… misery actually does love company. How many times have you sat back and dwelled in your own pity party? You invite yourself to your own table of sadness as you sit there all alone festering up the pain. You not only conjure up your own pain, but you ruin an opportunity to undo every attack that tried to attach itself to you. That's right, you are the one creating the attack. By doing this, you can also lose the opportunity at that moment to help move towards your destiny. This is a good time to reflect and self-identify all the unnecessary things that you view as negative.

Did you know that your identity was God created? According to *Jeremiah 1:5 (NIV)* the bible says, *"Before I formed you in the womb I knew you, and before you were born, I set you apart; I appointed you as a prophet to the nations."* Therefore, staying under any attack that someone has tried to bring you allows you to lose who God said you are. So, don't allow others to take away your identification. It's time to take a stand and say, "I wish a devil would," because that is the type of stance you have to take to defeat your giant.

Satan is a master in putting it directly in front of you to concentrate on the negative instead of all the good coming your way. A giant can be anything that holds your life hostage. One of my giants was anxiety or panic attacks. I remember when panic attacks were attacking my body, and my mind was in an unsafe place. That was my giant at the time. All kinds of turmoil were taking place within my own body, and I was allowing my mind to control it. That was all I could think about. Therefore, because I kept feeding into it, that giant became my focus. I came to understand that I was my own enemy because I was allowing my mind to stay under attack.

What does this mean? Let us first look at the definition of panic attacks. According to the Webster dictionary, a panic attack is, "a sudden feeling of acute and disabling anxiety." Now we know that the Bible speaks against anxiety according to *Philippians 4:6 (ESV) saying, "Do not be anxious about anything, but in everything by prayer and supplication…"* So, what was I worrying about? It was every symptom that worrying put on my body because, oftentimes, my mind would start to spiral out of control as I dwelled on the symptoms that I felt. One symptom would appear and once I fed into it with my thoughts, another symptom appeared. Do you get the picture? During this time, I found myself in a debilitative state; whatever I was feeling at the moment, put a fear over my body that was indescribable. So, I was stuck in a moment of despair as the distraction brought on by my own mind created my giant. Although, it was only a mere fraction of time, I felt helpless.

And that, my friend, is where Satan wants us to be. He is keeping us in dark places instead of the wonderful light that God has provided, and this helps to create your own pity party. God said it is time to start over; so, the attacks placed before you, will not have an effect on you. Our minds can either keep us in darkness or provide us with that wonderful light God provides. Something as simple as altering your chain of thought can change your outcome.

When peace shows up, and knocks at your door, grab hold of it and hold it tightly; because from this point on, you have choices to make. It's "mind over matter," as they say, and your life matters. The Bible speaks of this in *John 14:27 (ESV)*, which says *"And the peace of God, which transcends all understanding, will guard your hearts and your minds in Christ Jesus."* When you focus on all the attacks in your life and call them out for who or what they are, you will be able to undo all the attacks that stand before you.

I have given you an example of one of my giants, what are yours? Don't allow your mind to put you in a place of darkness. You have to focus on the word of God and allow your seed of faith to dwell inside of you to push out all the evilness that lurks to find us vulnerable, and invite peace in. Call out by name those things that are keeping you in a dark place and cast them down according to the word of God. *Ephesians 6:10 (NIV) tells us to, put on the full armor of God, and verse 12 tells us that our "struggle is not against flesh and blood, but against the rulers, against the authorities, against the powers of this dark world, and against the spiritual forces of the evil in heavenly realms."* We must start saying to everything that has us bound, "I cast you down in the name of Jesus," just as the Bible instructs us to do.

We must speak directly to the situation as if it was an actual giant. Our giants can show up in many forms and can be physical or mental. These things will no longer have power over our minds when we stand in agreement with the word of God. You can't constantly keep your mind in a dark place and expect to be healed from anything, including trauma. Fear is the opposite of who God is, and because God does not present himself with fear, cast it out. Anything that is not of God you have the power to cast out of your life. Therefore, as *Ephesians 11 (NIV)says, "Put on the full armor of God, so that you can take your stand against the devil's schemes."* It is necessary to let go of all the leftovers from life that causes ill effects, and know that they mean us no good. Our bodies have to be under renovation like rebuilding or tearing down an old house to restore it. All of our inner beings have to be transformed from the inside out in order to come from under the destruction of our minds. We must start to pull down the strongholds of our own minds.

2 Corinthians (NKJV) says, "For the weapons of our warfare are not carnal but mighty in God for pulling down strongholds." What does this line of scripture mean? I believe it is telling us to take a hold of every negative thought, immediately, and cast it out, or cast down anyone that comes your way with negativity because it is out of God's order. This is where we have to depend on our strength because, as stated above, we are not fighting against flesh and blood, but it's a spiritual warfare we are coming against. I also believe if we decide to go about life without the instructions of God's written word, we allow the attacks of the enemy to take control.

We have heard the saying, "when I look back over my life…" Well, when I do this, I see all the craziness that happened to me when I did not allow God to work in my life. All the craziness is what helped me develop, it put me on the track of forgiveness and helped me make better choices on how my life would be going forward. Don't allow your mind to stay in places that were not meant for you in the first place. We must reach for higher in order to stand at our highest. By doing this, you become aware of your surroundings and can cut so much off at the pass before it comes near you. Learn to trust your instincts and if it does not feel right, then it probably isn't. In addition, trust in your own mind by allowing itself to heal from any controversy that presents itself as your giant.

Reflection: Learn how to relax and know that God is with you. Once you have been attacked by life, know that you can undo it. Never stay in a place of disappointment. In addition, don't let the storms of life become your biggest regrets while learning how to calm them. *Mark: 4:38-39 (NIV) "Jesus was in the stern, sleeping on a cushion. The disciples woke him and said to him, "Teacher, don't you care if we drown?" He Got up, rebuked the* *wind, and said to the waves, "Quiet! Be still!" Then the wind died down and it was completely calm.*

CHAPTER 11: ONE LIFE TO LIVE

Your life is what you make it, so how you show up in it is of importance. Everything about who you are is just as valuable as the next person. I must salute a woman that shows up with so much confidence but doesn't shift the other woman's crown. Grown women actually show how powerful it is that each of us can be so brilliant in our own light that we don't overshadow anyone else's. We must know that God created each of us to have a space of our own while sharing space with someone else. We must not dim each other's light because there is room for us all. Just like the ocean that doesn't cross its boundaries that God sat for it, neither will we. That's right because we were given our own life to live and our territory also has a set space. Don't become a negative Nancy by deliberately trying to destroy someone else's life. Women should be prepared to share their strength with one another. Instead, we find ourselves in competition with one another. Life is precious, and since we all have only one, each day should be lived as if it were our last. It's crucial to perfect it in such a way that it does not hinder anyone else. There are so many challenges that we deal with; we must stay focused on all our own stuff.

After all the trauma in my life as a child, teenager, and as an adult, I can honestly say that I have had enough of life's challenges. There were times when I did not think I was going to be here because of someone else's actions. How is it that people think they have the right to either try and take someone's life or try and alter it in some type of way? Making better choices should be our goal to living our best life. Our lives should be full of a love language that is consistent with God's love. After all, we are all we got, and each one of us is irreplaceable.

So, ask yourself, if today was your last day on earth, would you be happy with who you are? Would you create better memories, or will you become someone else's strength? Ask yourself this question; would you be happy with where you decided to put all of your energy? This is a time to reflect on where you are. Can you benefit in life where you stand? The choices I made early in my life took me on a path of destruction in so many ways, but after seeking God's voice, I changed my choices. I felt better about myself when I decided to help others along the way. Others that have found themselves in similar situations as me. I said it before that we are strong in numbers. It's much easier to assist someone than to walk alone.

How was it even possible for me to walk alone in my own shoes? The shoes that were full of shame, abuse, and all the issues of my life prior to today were extremely difficult. It was as if a giant billboard that displayed everything about me was placed on a stand for all to see without me speaking a word. It kept me constantly falling over as if I was wearing heels constantly, like walking on the cracks of a sidewalk, for example, because I could not keep my balance. Each crack that I stumbled upon, revealed the history of my past.

Allowing someone to control my destiny, as stated in the previous chapter, almost ended my life here on earth. Once I realized that my past no longer served God's purpose for me, it was ultimately okay to let go of people, places, and things that did not align with my assignment. Life should not be about perfecting everything, but about progression. If you are not learning you are not growing, and it's that simple. It is important to decide, for your own peace, whether you are willing to lose yourself in order to please others. People that are only with you to distract you have to be sent on their way as you realize some people you just can't help.

Let's think of it this way; when we allow God to order our steps, according to *Psalm 119:133-136*, then pleasing people becomes a thing of the past, which means the pleasing spirit is dead. Yes, put up your emotional-block, because that pleasing spirit has now been deactivated. It is called, having up all your peace guards, and having your boundaries set, to maintain that peace.

I remember how I felt when I was shunned by my father, and it did not make me feel whole. I had to be someone else just to be in his presence because of the fear in my heart when I was around him. I was a broken child that allowed all kinds of unhealthy energy in my life. So, unless you let go of the child in you, things will never change. Without knowing it, by putting away their pain, children are often forgiving no matter what is done to them.

There are also adults that you may know who have held onto their trauma from their childhood, and they will hold you, and others, hostage because of it. Don't do it because you carry too much on your own! It is too much to live theirs and yours too. After all, it's not until the realization hits you that what you saw, and let go of as a child, manifested into trauma as an adult, making you relive it until you recognize it for what it was. Learning early in life that life is what you make it, will help you live up to your full potential, so you don't have to give up your energy to someone who inflicted pain early on. So, let's just call them *the remembered people*, because they constantly say, "don't you remember when," as they constantly bring up your past. Those who refuse to let go of yesterday do not belong in your present. We must learn early about negative emotions that will try and counter anything good that we learn or feel, if we do this. Now, as an adult, it is up to us to decide who we allow in our circle to maintain our sanity and to receive the love that we need.

Always keep your crown handy so you can be prepared to show others you are worthy when they refuse to apologize for wrongdoing. Sometimes you have to accept the apology that you will never receive from someone that hurt you to step into a clean space. Never be afraid to let go; because if you are afraid of someone, then your peace is taken away and they will hold a shadow of darkness over you as if you are still living in trauma. So, you must choose to let go.

I no longer choose to please people to make someone else feel validated. I cannot be the person who is being gaslighted by always worrying about someone else's manipulation. It makes it a one-sided relationship because the other person is constantly thinking about themselves. Allow your past only to be used as a blueprint to never go through it again, but not to be used against you as something you put up with.

Say to yourself, "my childhood trauma will not dictate what my future will be." The toxicity that was there when I was a child, when my parents raised me, can't be the reason I overcompensate for others. It should be how you choose to show up when pressure is applied in your life. Pressure often comes with the territory when we decide to follow God because many people will fall by the wayside, and that sometimes stings. When trying to people-please, know that you will always find yourself falling short because you have not removed yourself from the equation. You have total control of who comes into your life now, so take control.

I remember visiting my father as a little girl when my parents finally divorced, I was longing for him to show me love, but as a little girl, I did not understand the word "love" as demonstrated by the word of God. I was acting off emotions based on how I felt at the time. Therefore, it did not matter how bad he made me feel. All I knew, at the time, was that I needed him. It is important for us when we are raising our children to help them understand good and bad love.

Not everyone that speaks on love actually knows the meaning of it in terms of how to show it in their actions. *1*

John 4:8 (NIV) states, *"Whoever does not love does not know God, because God is love."* Therefore, in our human form, it is almost impossible to love in this way because He loves us unconditionally with every fault that we ever have on full display. Indeed, everything that we have ever done in life, according to His word, is on full display; yet, He loves us anyway. However, in our human nature, we will automatically hold things against one another that could impact our relationships moving forward. God has given us a blueprint on how to love one another, but sin has cast a major shadow on everyone. He is the perfect blueprint.

Each day will bring about its challenges, yet we will consciously hold on to our yesteryears without thinking about the cause and effect of it. After all, it wasn't until I wrote down my past that I realized that I was not being true to myself because of what I was holding on to. When you live your past, then your past is where you will stay. Oftentimes, our past was a lonely dark place, so what would be the benefit of holding on to it? There are more benefits to making amends with the hurts and pains than there are to holding on to them. We deny ourselves the opportunity for a new beginning that each day brings by hanging onto what yesterday was. Even when our days are good, there is an opportunity to improve on them.

The year twenty-twenty should have taught us that, in an instant, life could change, and how we view ourselves should be a moment of reflection. It was the beginning of a virus that caused the world to shut down and should have helped us see how precious life could be. It is an opportunity to learn how to balance our frustrations as well as our fears. We learned to live differently while sheltered from the chaos of the world. We were forced to live within the compound of our own homes. Many of us got to see the individuals that we were while keeping out the noise of others. We figured out what and who meant the most and let go of things and those that didn't matter. There is still so much chaos dealing with Covid-19 and we are still trying to fit others back into our lives who just should not be there. Understand that it is okay to, "let go and let God," as they say. This life that was given to us is more than just one life because it is a chance to create many memories while creating new ones that are beneficial to our souls. Continue to keep out the distractions and let them move on hastily while you comfort and protect yourself slowly.

Reflection: We have to decide how we show up for ourselves in front of all to see. The distractions that may come should only be temporary because we are the ones that can perform its completion. It's okay to help others along the way as long as they have your best interest in mind. *1 Corinthians 7:35 (NLT) "I am saying this for your benefit, not to place restrictions on you."*

CHAPTER 12: STEPPING INTO MY NEW *THANG*; WHEN A WOMAN IS FED UP

There is power in having conversations with people that are on your level, but there is also power in having conversations with people that think they are above you. We are fed up with the system that is trying to tear us down. So, look out world because women have now discovered a new *thang* about themselves and are more energized than ever before. What does this mean? We won't allow others to tear us down any longer as we are willing to fight for the cause.

Do you realize how many people you are around, or that you spend time with, that will judge you based on the level you have decided to reach, instead of where you came from? That's because people think that they don't have to invest fully in who you are. Let me explain. Oftentimes, we can meet people who will try and snatch out of you what will help them while pushing you aside. They are not even trying to stand with you, or even encourage you, and most of the time, will not show up for you. It's like being in a relationship where you are not valued completely, and therefore, they don't have to invest in all of you.

You can't just give fifty percent of yourself in a relationship and expect to survive because most of what you will receive will not be someone's best. They can just throw something at you and say I gave you what I have, but that can be the worst part of who they are. I experienced that in my last marriage. When I was giving all that I had, I basically received nothing in return. It has to be one hundred percent equal or you're not giving your all. Whoever said that giving half of yourself is enough, got it wrong. In fact, they were very wrong. That means that you won't even try to show up completely. Your attitude about life will be short-lived because you think that what you provide is enough in order to survive in society. Eighty percent isn't even enough. It's like that cup half full *thang* and you trying to decide which one best suit your lifestyle. Well, honey, it is time to step into your new *thang* because it's all or nothing. Maybe you were the one that only provided half of you and then only received half back. Well, you get what you give. How does that make you feel?

There is a lot of loneliness in an unfilled cup, and I know you felt the impact of it. There can be a lot of unfulfilled passion in an unfilled cup as well. Personally, I have decided I am worth everything and as I step into my new *thang,* one hundred percent is all I will accept. My cup has to be "overflowing" as written in scripture, according to (*Psalm 23*). It is important for me to have more than enough. Who ever thought that receiving half of something is a form of completion is nuts! When God created the world, he did it completely! It wasn't a partial completion. He gave one hundred percent of Himself in order to get it done. Now we are experiencing His marvelous work. Where would we be if He would not have given all of Himself? The world would be a disaster. Scripture says, *"Six days shall work be done: but the seventh day is the sabbath of rest." Leviticus 23:3 (ESV).* He did not stop at day three which would have been about fifty percent. He completed His task, and we reap the benefits of it, and then He rested. We have to put in the work to become complete, and that includes in a relationship. I will never accept half of someone. I want it all. This tells me that if we don't put our full self into something, we will accept something incomplete. So, whatever we do, we have to give our all-in order to become complete or fulfilled. Half of anything is less than and is not enough.

Let's look at dieting, for example. They say to eat half portions to lose weight so maybe that's fifty percent of a meal, but you are not satisfied at that moment. So, what do you do? You will then decide to consume the other fifty percent in order to feel satisfied. So instead, consume something that will be more satisfying and healthier and take in all of it, not just half. It's the same in relationships as we seek to find a healthy relationship, whether it's a friendship, or a partner, they should be able to receive wholeness from you. Then you, in turn, will want and receive wholeness as well. We should be fed up with anything that is not of substance, anyway. Therefore, we should want all of everything, or nothing at all, because there is no wholeness there. When a woman is fed up with all the nonsense that is presented to her, look out, because she has realized that you are not totally invested in her. Most often, there is no turning back to retrieve the other fifty percent when she becomes focused and fed up. Things that have hurt her will no longer be tolerated and will become a thing of the past as she has been given a path forward.

I recall, when in the abusive relationship, I decided that running was no longer an option. It was going to be him or me. Yes, I prepared myself for battle. When we get to a point that it's time to fight, then everything is suddenly seen differently. A shift is coming as our demands become greater because we are looking for new things that will make us whole, and that's a form of us feeling complete. Don't ever accept anything less than your worth because you will become exhausted trying to hold on to it. In addition, don't allow someone to take from you what they never put in. Use your energy to push past all the, "you can't do it by yourself people." A healthy relationship cannot be received from a half-give person. Once you understand that you are over being unfilled with what someone else is trying to get from you, then being unresponsive to the big lie becomes easy. They may have lied about wanting a real friendship or relationship with you because they were just trying to get something from you to up their game. You become the one that was unfulfilled.

Did you know that there are also gaps between the fifty percent given to you? You will have many moments of unfulfillment. This will allow moments of sadness and feelings of rejection which may lead to your loneliness.

Reflect back to moments in your life where you felt these things and you will see your gaps. Women are more than what we allow someone to take out of us because everything we ever hoped for can be right at our fingertips. It is only a matter of reaching and finding all that was left out or taken. Just like every woman before us had to fight to be seen, so will we. The difference is, now we are more prepared for the fight. We can see right through you because they taught us well. Our standards should be high when trusting others to complete us or add to us. Don't let someone take away the importance of giving one hundred percent of themselves to you. It's either all or nothing, and not a half full cup or a half empty cup, because in reality, it's the same. Either way leaves too much room for emptiness to enter and will leave you with scars that may last a lifetime. You can find joy when stepping out into your new *thang* by just completing yourself.

People will not be able to tear down the barrier you have created for yourself no matter how hard they try. They can't break what they can't penetrate, and they definitely won't be able to break your soul. Just forgive them and have them go on their merry way. However, they will be able to view you from the outside as you remain untouchable. So, as you continue to reach for higher levels, people will draw to you like a magnet but won't be able to snatch out of you what made you who you are because you have put up all your defense guards. Learn how to bow out gracefully while walking in fullness.

Reflection: Life can become what you make it as you reach for a set goal. Don't allow what is offered to become something accepted to be a form of completion for you. You are worthy of all your praise. *Psalm 3:3 (NKJV) "But You, O Lord, are a shield for me, my glory and the One who lifts up my head."*

CHAPTER 13: A STRANGER IN MY HOUSE

Protect you at all costs! We can't become comfortable or complacent to destruction within our own homes or outside of it, for that matter. The house that you have to pull, drag, and sometimes carry in order to get to the next place, is shunned by the negativity of the world. The very world who doesn't see you as you should be seen. The house that has become accustomed to someone else's view of itself. This house is you! Never lose sight of who you are, and don't let anyone tear you down.

Also, never put yourself in a place of becoming uncomfortable with who you are. Will you allow you to be destroyed? You can become a stranger to yourself if you allow others to destroy those things that you built. People will try and tear down the very essence of your soul if you let them. *1 Corinthians 3:16-17 (NIV)* speaks about our bodies being God's temple, so it is important to protect them because scripture says it's sacred. We must position ourselves higher in life to receive what has already been given. We, as children of God, have been given a process to allow the manifestation that is God-given to show in us for our house to stand. We have to be humble, obedient, and stay in the process that God has intended for us. In order not to become a stranger to yourself, you have to keep your own house clean. Sweep through every part that is dusty so you can see what has been destroyed to replace it with new. The things that are unrecognizable, get rid of, in order to not become estranged from the best part of you. Safeguard your stronghold and keep the master key so you can maneuver when needed; you are the one in charge. Keep your mind healthy at all times by not allowing distractions to take hold. Mental health should become a major priority to detach from the worst part of the world. While society appears to be adjusting to violence, our minds should be adjusting to peace. It is very imperative that we focus on what we draw into our thoughts as we give ourselves permission to reclaim what is ours. Do you even recognize yourself at this point? If not, it's okay to change. When we decide to carry things of unimportance with us, we become unrecognizable to ourselves.

Ultimately, what we decide to plant inside us will be what shows on the outside. We then reap what we sew. Think about it; it's like planting a garden, but not just any garden. You must be particular about what you want planted. Once you choose it, you then plant it; but for it to flourish or develop, you must water it, love it, and shelter it. If you don't give the seed what it needs to develop, it will die. It is the same thing that you plant inside of your mind; the more you feed it negativity, the more negative you become. If you stop feeding it, then the negativity will die.

It's like you have to lose yourself in order to find yourself. You must become a complete stranger to who you were in order to gain respect to who you are in your own house. The human part of you no longer exists, in many ways, if you become complacent with your feelings. Learning about each physical attribute that is sustained within you would be helpful to your own understanding of self. Ask yourself a couple of questions. What does your body feel like when it is stressed? What does your body feel like when it is at peace? Learn the difference between the two. Then ask yourself which one you prefer. It's almost like you are searching for your inner child because children have a place of innocence. You must remember the part of you that did not judge in any way but simply accepted what it was because that becomes the best of you.

Rejection is not a part of your psyche as a very young child because you don't usually have knowledge of it. Once you are bruised, damaged, or wounded is when the concept of life takes on a new meaning. Your pureness has now been displaced by what we have allowed to stain us. Stains are hard to get rid of because it takes a lot of scrubbing and the right ingredients to remove them. You are now in a war with yourself from within as you try to clean away the waste. It's time to clean your house from the strange things that try to take up space within you. You have become used to the insecurities based on what you have allowed in. Sweep through and guard every part that is valuable and precious to you so you can protect the delicate parts that strengthen you. Have the same compassion for yourself that you would have for a stranger in need.

Allow people to see you where you are while understanding your vision. Once I started to realize that it was easier to change everything around me, including the negative thoughts, I began to put in the work to change my circumstances. Everything about me became necessary, but it didn't help if I didn't work on my mind, and it didn't take me long to realize that sometimes in my life, I was a stranger to myself, and I didn't quite understand it. Learn who you are and separate yourself from the distractions. Always keep in mind that your house, the person that you carry and fight for each day, are of importance, to not just you, but everyone you come in contact with. Make yourself a priority to maintain your inner being. Learn to separate the stranger in you and make peace with the renewed you. Make an example of your strength, your character, and your courage so you will have the desires of your heart by not letting others distract you. There will never be a better example of you, than you. So, connect to your outside, as well as your inside, in order to become familiar with who you are. Your relationship with self will be the best that you will ever have.

Reflection: They say, *life is but a dream*, so dream big. Don't become complacent to the strangers you allow in your house because each one will be valuable to who you are. *Deuteronomy 10:19 (NRSV) "You shall also love the stranger, for you were strangers in the land of Egypt."*

CHAPTER 14: I BEAR MANY FACES; BECOME THE BRAND

U nderstanding what broken feels like comes from the shadows of my own life. I had become the face of a brand that bore the many faces of life's challenges, and I did not realize it while going through my journey called, life. How is it that what we carry, not only affects us individually, but collectively, in some cases? We, as women, must realize that while we feel alone and isolated, God is faithful to carry us through. Scripture says, *"And God is faithful, and he will not let you be tempted beyond what you can bear."* according to *1 Corinthians 10:13 (NIV)* this scripture speaks volumes because God's word is His promise to us. However, when I look back over my own life, there are so many faces attached to me that it's scary, at best.

How is it that some of us will go through, or over, many mountains in life, while others don't? In the midst of my valleys, I did not recognize that I was going through any at all because it was presented as normal; so, don't let someone else's normal become yours. Don't stay in the valley because it's too deep and steep, and quite lonely. Sure, the struggles were real, and frustrations were many, but God was always there, even when I was in it. He is always waiting to assist you if, and when, you decide to remove yourself so He can take over. This is a time that you must become intentional about life. I learned that it's okay to see through all the pain while learning along the way. Ultimately, I had to love myself in my lows while trying to reach my highs. How can you switch from the many faces that have attached themselves to you? After all, the faces I bore were of pain, abandonment, abuse, and loneliness, and while there are many more, death was the one that tried to attach itself to me. Eventually, my body would start to fail me, not once, but twice. The first time was when a knife was put in my back, and the second was when I ended up in the hospital not knowing who I was. Was there an intervention from God as to why I am still amongst the living, and furthermore is there still work for me to do? Absolutely, because God was in the midst of my struggles, my valleys, and He stood at every mountain. I believe it's because of my purpose I am still here.

Indeed, the struggles were real, but my most astonishing testament is that God never wavered from His word. That is my most inspiring moment because this is when I learned that He speaks to us through His word. How is it that, early on, I did not know that while in those challenging times, He was with me, initially? How did I know to hold on? That is why it is so important to change your life exactly where you stand because that's when you realize, God has got you.

Throughout life lessons, there are things that we are to learn from, and that is not to repeat the same thing that causes us pain. Why should we want to keep ourselves there? Sure, pain can be inevitable in certain situations that we have no control over, but the things that we can control, we must. Since pain is one of the faces that was attached to me very early in life, it was hard to figure out what it was. For example, once I figured out that whatever broke my heart, caused me pain outside of the physical pain, I had to stay away from it. It was as if I had to transition myself to a greater height in order to stand above what would no longer hurt me. Ultimately, the decision was mine because while transitioning to greater, nothing beneath the level of God was permitted. I had to officially apologize to myself, as well, for not recognizing that I was the one causing some of my internal pain by simply allowing it to exist in the first place.

How is it that we see and feel toxicity but allow it to continue? Even though I bear so many faces, so do the people that try to come into our lives. You can actually feel the toxic energy coming straight at you. They know they are out to deceive you from the beginning, but you will not see a face of deception at first glance. Those types of people are so used to it that they feel you are the toxic one. They will actually do something to get you angry and while you are upset about the situation, they get mad at you for being mad at them for something they did. Did you catch all of that? They will never recognize or even admit to any fault. You will also never hear an apology from them, and you will be the one who wronged them. This is when you should step back and evaluate their importance in your life. It's okay, and sometimes necessary, to love from a distance. That is when it also becomes necessary to move about differently when in the presence of those type of people. Most of their actions won't be intentional but the majority of the time, it is. Either way, don't expect an apology.

While becoming a brand of the many faces that most of society experiences, none will be like your own personal experience. Abandonment from my father is a brand that I wish was very different because I needed him throughout my life. Rejection is a brand that no one, especially a young child, should ever experience. Wearing the brand of abuse should never have happened and should not happen to anyone at any time. While there are countless more, brands are something that many should never have to wear. Although they may be invisible to the naked eye to those looking in, it will remain a visible brand to those that suffer in silence.

Across the world, women today are stronger than ever, and although the brands that we wear were meant to destroy us, we are still here. We stand in the gap against the labels and titles that have tried to shame many of us because of what we went through. Ultimately, we have learned that healing comes from accepting who we have become by holding on to one another. When we unite under one umbrella, so to speak, we are mighty in numbers. We learn to be gentle and less aggressive while restructuring the brands we have come accustomed to wearing. We then choose to bear the face of women that have shown themselves and proved throughout history that they are strong, yet loving. Thereby, putting aside all the hurts in order to let go of some of our independence that we graciously carry while investing in ourselves. We also will choose to brand ourselves with only positive vibes so that what we put out, we will then receive.

Reflection: We are more than our outwardly appearance, and all that we hold inside us is bigger than any brand that attaches itself to us. Tell'em you are fearfully and wonderfully made, tell'em you're beautiful, tell'em nothing can stop you, tell'em you are branded by the best, tell'em you were created by the King. *Genesis 1:27 (NIV) "So God created mankind in his image, in the image of God he created them; male and female he created them."* Tell'em.

Daisy Arness Marrs

CHAPTER 15: LIFE IS JUST A REHEARSAL; FINAL CURTAIN CALL

Have you ever done something or allowed something to happen and regretted it not long after? If you had the opportunity, what would you go back and change in your life? I can actually say that when I got married the first time, it never should have happened, and is a moment of regret. When we regret something and can't go back and make it right, we move forward never repeating the same thing. In my mature mind now, I can say that was the beginning of my life's rehearsal, and my performance was simply not up to par. When we show up, we should be prepared to do life the best we can, but then we realize everything that we rehearsed for was a mess. Your audience saw something that was shocking. No one actually gets it right the first time. Life should be how we make it, right? How will the best of you show up when you think you are prepared to do your final curtain call? Will your performance be one of elegance or require many repeat performances? We have finally figured out that our rehearsal was a mess when the curtain closed and was a disaster in front of all to see. I was in charge at that very moment but did not think about what the rest of my life would be like because of the immaturity of my mind. I was also in charge of my own storyline and all the drama that existed in my life; from that moment on, I controlled the script. The very first time that I was abused, I could have rewritten the direction of my own life and moved beyond all the drama that was put before me. How is it that we allow others to rewrite our scripts? I should have walked away, but instead, I allowed the direction from my youth to narrate my first rehearsal when put in charge. When we are put in charge, an opportunity is given to us to perfect it. Many of us can think back as early as yesterday or as far back as thirty years ago, and realize that mistakes were made, mishaps were done, things were said, and then say, "I wish I would have done it differently." What would you do differently if you could map out your own scenes? How will you select your cast members? How many scenes will you have? Since we are all given choices to make, every single day given should be our best rehearsal.

Think about it! Each day should bring about change, and we should have learned from the day before. According to Wikipedia, the definition for rehearsal is "a practice or trial performance of a play or other work for later public performance." Therefore, we are given time to rehearse our lives until we get it right, and we can change our direction at any moment in order to have a great performance. Balancing each and every challenge that comes our way is simply a dress rehearsal until our last breath is taken. Given this, how will you show up each day? Will you bring all of yesterday into today? How you show up for yourself each day given, will be up to you to decide. Rehearsals are what we do until we can get something right to perfect something like life. We actually write our own chapters in life and create our own characters when we invite someone into our lives. That's right, we are the producers, editors, and writers. We use our voices to narrate each and every second of the day that we choose to show up. Although we may have made plans for tomorrow, next week, or even next year, the pages are basically empty because we simply don't know when our last rehearsal will be.

Can you even write a script to present to others that would allow you to show up without some disappointments? The opportunity that would have you without flaws and so many mistakes that would not leave you embarrassed. Taking the lead in your own life's rehearsal is how you can show up in a positive way. Actually, because we are human and everyone makes mistakes, it's a continuous process. *James 3:2 (NIV) states, "We all stumble in many ways. Anyone who is never at fault in what they say is perfect, able to keep their whole body in check."* What I get from this scripture is that there is no perfect man that walks this earth because Jesus was the only one. We are going to mess it up. Ultimately, we know life is a practice session each and every day. You can practice your actions numerous times, and still get them wrong. Once I figured out that I did not like the way my life was going, I trashed the first script and rewrote it. Characters had to be changed because they could not move forward in my production. In fact, the entire performance had to be redone. We have to start trusting God with our tomorrow in order to perfect today. Our fate has already been established from the very beginning of time on that fateful day that Eve chose to defy the word of God; so, it is important to be the best director you can be. As the director, understand that it's necessary to bring a notebook and pencil with you because you will be doing a lot of erasing and rewriting. Like the first part of my life was a wreck, so will yours be, if you don't perfect your script. So, bring a towel with you, also, because there will be a lot of sweat and tears, honey. You will also feel drained early on, so be prepared to adjust your schedule. I've learned that as a general rule, a rehearsal has four main stages according to www.stagemilk.com (Guide to a Successful Rehearsal Process-Stagemilk). They are Understanding, Exploration, Practice, and Presentation. So, as long as we understand from the start that a lot of patience and time is required during this process, we should adjust our schedules accordingly.

Exploring is a time when we should get excited because things start to unfold in our lives because we should be creating something different. It's as if we are manifesting something before our very eyes. However, as we start to practice things in our lives, things begin to unfold because we find that there are many obstacles along the way, and we are no longer at the beginning stage. We should have been more aware at this point in rehearsal. We also understand that we can't do it like we did it the first time and realize that there is still time to perfect it. Now it's time to present yourself and be consistent in how your presentation will be seen. You prepare your run of the show, and everything will be laid out in front of you. Your production will be on full display and people will be watching everything you do. So, remember those you invite in are a part of the characters that you have created. Your run of the show should include your audience in your script because everywhere you go in life, from this point on, will be judged. Will you be ready to raise the curtain on your life to be put on full display for the world to see? Will you shy away from the characters you chose? We can rehearse as often as we want, but we are basically programmed by our own choices to still get it wrong because of the sinful nature we all have, according to *Romans 3:23*. Don't allow the sinful nature of others to distract your progress. Life is just a rehearsal, and we can choose to wake up each day and choose to practice each moment until we get it right.

Ultimately, we can show ourselves approval by way of our appearance. There is a saying that, practice makes perfect, and it's up to us to practice living in a positive way, versus negatively. Who will be in charge of your rehearsal? How will you prepare yourself during practice? Details will emerge during your lifetime that will either make you out to be a villain or a martyr to society. Let your life rehearsal become a major part of your production company. Each of us has an opportunity to show ourselves approval because as long as we have breath in our bodies, we have a chance for change. Who will be in charge of the clothes you wear, the way you speak, and all of your practice sessions? There is no one rooting for you more than God, and He will always be your greatest cheerleader. If you wake up every day and remember that then each dress rehearsal will be your best. You will also expect to be able to show up to be the very best that you can be. When you expect something different, when you put your best foot forward, you will be able to be conscious of every curtain call. Therefore, it is important to perform at your greatest in order to transition to being your best. You should be able to notice your own transition from the beginning of rehearsal until your last, and when that final curtain closes, the choice is up to you.

Reflection: Don't allow life to pass you by as if you are a mere reflection of it. Live each day as if it were your last because no one knows when your final curtain will close, so choose your characters wisely. *Matthew24:36 (NIV), "But about that day or hour no one knows, not even the angels in heaven, nor the Son, but only the Father."*

THE SOUL OF A WOMAN

Daisy Arness Marrs

ABOUT THE AUTHOR

DAISY ARNESS MARRS

Daisy Arness Marrs is the Founder/CEO of A-Way-Out Ministries, Inc. She lives in Indianapolis, Indiana with her husband, children, and grandchildren. As an Advocate for Domestic Violence, she is passionate about the work she does in her community by being a voice for those that have experienced Domestic Violence. As a survivor herself Daisy understands that advocacy is necessary to find your path forward. She has an initiative called *"Framed by Violence"* as well as *"One Voice Indy"* which sheds light on how communities have been impacted by violence. Her first book released in September 2021 received an award related to woman issues. Daisy is also a Nurse, Licensed Cosmetologist and received her degree in Christian Ministry from Indiana Wesleyan University in May 2020. You can find her story "Domestic Terror the Daisy Marrs Story" on YouTube.

THE SOUL OF A WOMAN

Enhanced
DNA
DEVELOP. NURTURE. ACHIEVE.
Publishing Division

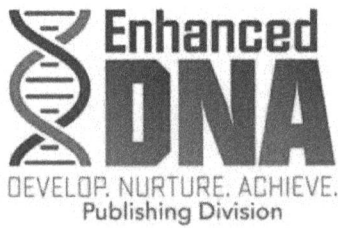

www.EnhancedDNAPublishing.com
info@EnhancedDNA1.com

www.ingramcontent.com/pod-product-compliance
Lightning Source LLC
Chambersburg PA
CBHW070045100426
42740CB00013B/2799